Ecclesiology

The Church as Communion and Mission

Catholic Basics

A Pastoral Ministry Series

Morris Pelzel, Ph.D.

Thomas P. Walters, Ph.D.
Series Editor

NATIONAL CONFERENCE FOR
CATECHETAL LEADERSHIP

LOYOLAPRESS.
3441 N. ASHLAND AVENUE
CHICAGO, ILLINOIS 60657

NIHIL OBSTAT: Rev. Daniel J. Mahan, S.T.B., S.T.L.
Censor Librorum

IMPRIMATUR: Rev. Msgr. Joseph F. Schaedel
Vicar General/Moderator of the Curia

Given at Indianapolis, Indiana, on February 19, 2001

The *nihil obstat* and *imprimatur* are official declarations that a book is free of doctrinal and moral error. No implication is contained herein that those who have granted the *nihil obstat* and *imprimatur* agree with the content, opinions, or statements expressed.

Acknowledgments appearing on page 122 constitute a continuation of the copyright page.

Cover Design: Other Brother Design
Cover Illustration: Steve Snodgrass
Interior Illustrations: Other Brother Design

Library of Congress Cataloging-in-Publication Data

Pelzel, Morris
Ecclesiology : the church as communion and mission / Morris Pelzel.
p. cm. – (Catholic basics)
Rev. ed. of: The church as communion and mission.
Includes bibliographical references.
ISBN 0-8294-1726-5
1. Church. 2. Pastoral theology–Catholic Church. I. Pelzel, Morris.
Church as communion and mission. II. Title. III. Series.

BX1746 .P387 2001
262'.02–dc21
2001029696
CIP

ISBN: 0-8294-1726-5

Published by Loyola Press, 3441 N. Ashland Avenue, Chicago, Illinois 60657 U.S.A.
© 2002 The National Conference for Catechetical Leadership.

01   02   03   04   05   Bang   5   4   3   2   1

Ecclesiology

Table of Contents

About the Series   viii

Certification Standards: National Resources
    for Church Ministry   ix

Introduction   xi

CHAPTER 1: **A Vision of Church—
Communion and Mission**   1

"Communion" and "Mission" as a Framework for Ecclesiology   2

The Communion and Mission of the Trinity—Source of
    the Church's Communion and Mission   5

Unfolding the Vision—The Plan of This Book   7

Summary   11

For Reflection   11

CHAPTER 2: **The Church—Communion
of Disciples**   12

Communion—Bond of Life in the Church   15

Father, Son, and Spirit—A Life of Perfect Communion   17

We Are Invited to Share God's Life   18

Communion Among Members of the Church   20

The Parish—Communion of Households   21

The Diocese—Communion of Parishes   23

The Universal Church—Communion of Local Churches   24

Communion Beyond the Visible Church   26

The Church—Communion of Disciples   27

Summary   29

For Reflection   29

CHAPTER 3: **CHARISMS, MINISTRIES, AND STATES OF LIFE IN THE CHURCH**   30

The Common Status of the People of God   32

The Church Evolves Through History   35

The Correspondence of Charisms, Tasks, and Offices   37

States of Life in the Church—Laity, Clergy, and Religious   39

Summary   52

For Reflection   52

CHAPTER 4: **THE CHURCH—FORMED THROUGH WORD AND SACRAMENT**   53

The Word of God—In the Church, Above the Church   55

Advancing Toward the Plenitude of Divine Truth   56

The "Sense of the Faith" (*Sensus Fidei*)   58

The Whole Church, Learning and Teaching   60

Sacraments—Signifying and Sanctifying   63

The Church—Universal Sacrament of Salvation   65

Sacraments—By the Church, For the Church   66

Eucharistic Ecclesiology   67

Summary   70

For Reflection   71

CHAPTER 5: **THE MISSION OF THE CHURCH— EVANGELIZING CULTURES**   72

Evangelization—Deepest Identity of the Church   75

The Essential Moments of Evangelization   77

The New Evangelization   79

The Evangelization of Cultures   80

What Are Cultures?   82

Transforming the Cultures of the United States   84

The Inculturation of the Gospel and the Church   85

Summary   88

For Reflection   88

CHAPTER 6: THE MISSION OF THE CHURCH—
TRANSFORMING THE WORLD   89

The Church—In the World But Not of the World   91

The Church "in" the Modern World—*Gaudium et Spes*
and Beyond   93

What Is the "World"?   96

The World—Created for the Church   98

Catholic Social Teaching—Our Best Kept Secret   100

Summary   103

For Reflection   104

CHAPTER 7: THE CHURCH—ONE, HOLY,
CATHOLIC, APOSTOLIC   105

The Church—Holy in a Way That Can Never Fail   107

The Holiness of the Church—Genuine Though Imperfect   108

The Catholic Unity of the Church   111

Catholicity—The Fullness of Giving and Receiving   113

Summary   115

For Reflection   115

Conclusion   116

Abbreviations   117

Resources for Further Study   119

Acknowledgments   122

About the Author   123

About the Series

Catholic Basics: A Pastoral Ministry Series offers an in-depth yet accessible understanding of the fundamentals of the Catholic faith for adults, both those preparing for lay ministry and those interested in the topics for their own personal growth. The series helps readers explore the Catholic tradition and apply what they have learned to their lives and ministry situations. Each title offers a reliable introduction to a specific topic and provides a foundational understanding of the concepts.

Each book in the series presents a Catholic understanding of its topic as found in Scripture and the teachings of the Church. Each of the authors has paid special attention to the documents of the Second Vatican Council and the *Catechism of the Catholic Church*, so that further learning can be guided by these core resources.

Chapters conclude with study questions that may be used for small group review or for individual reflection. Additionally, suggestions for further reading offer dependable guides for extra study.

The initiative of the National Conference of Catechetical Leadership led to the development of an earlier version of this series. The indispensable contribution of the series editor, Dr. Thomas Walters, helped ensure that the concepts and ideas presented here are easily accessible to a wide audience.

Certification Standards: National Resources for Church Ministry

E ach book in this theology series relates to standards for theological competency identified in the resources listed below. Three national church ministry organizations provide standards for certification programs that serve their respective ministries. The standards were developed in collaboration with the United States Catholic Conference Commission on Certification and Accreditation. The fourth resource is the latest document, and it was developed to identify common goals of the three sets of standards.

Competency Based Certification Standards for Pastoral Ministers, Pastoral Associates and Parish Life Coordinators. Chicago: National Association for Lay Ministry, Inc. (NALM), 1994.

These standards address three roles found in pastoral ministry settings in the United States. The standards were the earliest to receive approval from the United States Catholic Conference Commission on Certification and Accreditation. Copies of the standards are available from the National Association for Lay Ministry, 5420 S. Cornell, Chicago, IL 60615-5604.

National Certification Standards for Professional Parish Directors of Religious Education. Washington, DC: National Conference for Catechetical Leadership, 1998.

NCCL developed standards to foster appropriate initial education and formation, as well as continuing personal and professional development, of those who serve as Directors of Religious Education. The standards address various areas of knowledge and the abilities needed in the personal, theological, and professional aspects of the ministry. Also included is a code of ethics for professional catechetical leaders. Available from the National Conference of Catechetical Leadership, 3021 Fourth Street NE, Washington, DC 20017-1102.

Competency-Based Standards for the Coordinator of Youth Ministry.
   Washington, DC: National Federation for Catholic Youth
   Ministry, 1996.

This document lays out the wide range of knowledge and skills that support ministry with young people as well as the successful leadership and organization of youth ministry wherever it may be situated. The standards are available from the National Federation for Catholic Youth Ministry, 415 Michigan Avenue NE, Suite 40, Washington, DC 20017-1518.

Merkt, Joseph T., ed. *Common Formation Goals for Ministry.* A joint
   publication of NALM, NFCYM, and NCCL, 2000.

Rev. Joseph Merkt compared the documentation of standards cited by three national organizations serving pastoral, youth, and catechetical ministries. The resulting statement of common goals identifies common ground for those who prepare persons for ministry as well as for the many people who wear multiple hats. Copies are available from NALM, NCCL, or NFCYM.

Introduction

This book is about the Church. Thus, it is about us because we are the Church. In the first place, however, this book is about God because we the Church are formed and sustained in our life by the presence and action of Jesus and the Holy Spirit, sent among us by God the Father. So the Church, as this book, is really about relationships, about connections, about mutual giving and receiving among persons, divine and human.

Ecclesiology: the Church as Communion and Mission is a theological study of the Church. It presents, therefore, an ecclesiology, that is, a theology of the Church. What is offered here reflects both our experience of being the Church and our hope for what we can become as Church. It is a vision that calls us to action.

This book was composed with particular reference to the *Catechism of the Catholic Church (CCC)* and the recently published *General Directory for Catechesis (GDC)*. Both of these sources are steeped with citations from and references to official Church documents, especially documents of the Second Vatican Council and subsequent statements. Readers will note that there are frequent references in this book to these documents as well as to other theological sources. The intention is to present a study of the Church that reflects the main perspectives and themes found in these authoritative teachings. At the same time, the book seeks to offer a presentation of themes and ideas that is somewhat original in its arrangement and expression. Readers are encouraged to go to the original source documents as well as to other studies of ecclesiology, such as those mentioned in the list of resources for further study.

I would like to thank Dr. Thomas Walters, a faculty colleague at Saint Meinrad School of Theology. Tom's encouragement and counsel have helped to sustain my confidence during the writing of this book. I thank Tom, his wife Rita, and Paul

Kaiser for reading the manuscript and offering candid and insightful observations. I hope that by following their suggestions I have made the book more lively and clear to read. Its shortcomings, nonetheless, remain my own.

I wish to dedicate the book to my family: my parents, Albert and Clara Pelzel; my brothers and sisters and their families; and my wife Pamela and our daughter Madeleine Rose. I have been most richly blessed to be a part of this "domestic Church."

CHAPTER 1

A Vision of Church— Communion and Mission

For most Catholics, the celebration of the Mass is the fullest experience of what it means to be Christian and what it means to be the Church. By gathering in the presence of God and one another, listening to the stories of salvation, and sharing the eucharistic bread and cup at the table of the Lord, we reaffirm our identity as Christians. Having thus celebrated the eucharistic Liturgy, we are then sent back into the world in order to live the Christian life and to proclaim the Christian message in our daily lives.

"Communion" and "Mission" as a Framework for Ecclesiology

This book is a theological study of the Church, that is, an ecclesiology. There is a rhythm at work in the eucharistic Liturgy and thus in the Christian life as a whole that provides us with a key insight for understanding the Church. In this dynamic movement of coming together and going forth, symbolized in the rites of gathering and dismissal that frame the Mass, we have the basic elements for a theology of the Church. In theological categories, those basic elements may be termed "communion" and "mission." Reflection upon our ongoing experience of communion and mission can thus provide us with a vision of what it means to be the Church.

By focusing on communion and mission as categories for understanding the Church, we will be following the vision of the Second Vatican Council. It has often been observed that the Church as such was the principal object of attention in the proceedings and documents of the Second Vatican Council. Previous ecumenical councils in the history of the Church had different focal points. For example, the earliest ecumenical councils— those held in the ancient cities of Nicea (325 A.D.), Constantinople (381), and Chalcedon (451)—concentrated on the question of how Christians should properly understand and speak of God and Jesus Christ. These councils produced our basic statements of faith regarding the Trinity and the full humanity and divinity of Christ. At the Second Vatican Council, by comparison, the primary issue for understanding was not the doctrine of God or the person of Christ but, rather, the nature and identity of the Church.

The Second Vatican Council produced sixteen documents, all of which to some degree pertain to the renewal of the life of the Church. Two documents in particular, though, reflect explicitly upon the Church: the *Dogmatic Constitution on the Church (Lumen Gentium, LG)* and the *Pastoral Constitution on the Church in the Modern World (Gaudium et Spes, GS)*. In issuing these two documents, the council decided to address the topic of the Church from two interrelated and complementary perspectives: the inner life of the Church *(ecclesia ad intra)* and the life of the Church in the world *(ecclesia ad extra)*.

Although these two perspectives may be distinguished conceptually, in concrete reality they can never be separated. Even in those moments when the Church seems most focused on its own internal life for example (in liturgy or catechesis), it is still in the world, and its members come to liturgy or catechesis from the context of their lives in the world. Correspondingly, in those moments when the Church seems most focused on involvement in the world (for example, in providing humanitarian aid or attempting to influence the direction of social policy), it can only be effective insofar as its activity springs from a community that has a vibrant and vital inner life.

We can understand these complementary perspectives of *Lumen Gentium* (the "inner" life of the Church) and *Gaudium et Spes* (the "outer" life of the Church) to correspond to our categories of communion and mission. The inner life of the Church is realized in the communion of its members with God and with one another. The outer life of the Church is its mission, realized in manifold ways, in the world. Both are necessary for a comprehensive understanding of the Church. More precisely, communion and mission cannot be understood apart from one another. In the words of Pope John Paul II:

> Communion and mission are profoundly connect-
> ed with each other, they interpenetrate and mutual-
> ly imply each other to the point that *communion rep-
> resents both the source and the fruit of mission: commun-
> ion gives rise to mission and mission is accomplished in
> communion.* It is always the one and the same Spirit
> who calls together and unifies the Church and
> sends her to preach the Gospel "to the ends of the
> earth" (Acts 1:8).
>
> (*On the Vocation and the Mission of
> the Lay Faithful in the Church and in the
> World [Christifideles Laici, CL]*, #32)

Thus the communion, the bond of relationship with God
and one another, that Christians experience in their daily lives
and most intensely in the eucharistic Liturgy, does not "close in
upon itself." Our life "inside" the Church is not a life insulated
from non-Christians and the secular world of the outside; rather,
it is precisely the experience to which we invite the entire world
to participate. As Christians we must not simply dwell in the
Church as a comfortable refuge of like-minded friends; we have
an imperative to always widen the circles of inclusion in our
communal life, ultimately "to the ends of the earth." The liturgical rite of dismissal at the end of Mass does not simply mean
"now the service is over, and you are permitted to leave"; rather,
it means "go into the world now, and live there what you have
just celebrated." The very word "Mass" comes from the Latin formula for the rite of dismissal—*Ite, missa est*—meaning, "Go, the
Mass is ended, be sent forth." So the words "Mass" and "mission"
come from the same source; thus, we cannot really understand
the Mass without seeing how it leads us to take up our mission
as Christians in the world. This is the true meaning of our being
"dis-missed" from the eucharistic Liturgy.

But what is this mission? Though it takes many forms, ultimately the goal of the Christian mission is to widen and enrich the
communion of the human family, to make it completely inclusive.

The goal is to broaden the eucharistic assembly. So from a Christian perspective, just as every gathering (communion) leads at some point to a sending forth (mission), so the purpose of going forth is to build up, to enhance, the experience of communion.

In official documents and in theological literature since the Second Vatican Council, there has been a growing agreement that "communion" is the category that best explains the essential nature of the Church. So there has been a flourishing of "communion ecclesiologies." Perhaps less prominent has been the insistence that "mission" is an equally important category for understanding the Church and that, indeed, one cannot fully understand "communion" in the Church without also understanding "mission." This is not to say that "mission" has not received a significant amount of attention but rather that the connection of "communion" and "mission" has not been reflected on in the same depth as has the concept "communion" in itself. So it is not unusual to see references to the nature and mission of the Church, which, while perhaps not technically inaccurate, could give the impression that the Church's mission in the world is not really part of its nature. It is more accurate to say that the Church's nature is missionary, or again that communion and mission together form the nature or essence of the Church.

The Communion and Mission of the Trinity—Source of the Church's Communion and Mission

In saying that the rhythm of communion and mission is what defines the Church, we are not just saying something about the Church. In fact, the reason we say that ecclesial life is defined by communion and mission is that these same realities are first of all characteristic of divine life. God is a communion of persons, each equal to one another and sharing a life of mutual giving and receiving. And, in the gracious and loving plan of God, this divine communion is opened up to the created world through the missions of the Son and the Spirit in the world. In other words, God the Father sends the Son and the Holy Spirit into the world in order to draw the human family into that family's own communion of life. Thus, at the beginning of *LG*, in paragraphs 2–4, the trinitarian basis for the unity (communion) of the Church is presented, with the following conclusion: "Thus the Church has been seen as 'a people made one with the unity of the Father, the Son and the Holy Spirit.'" (*LG*, #4, citing Thomas Aquinas, *Summa Theol.* III, q. 63, a. 2).

Likewise, early in the Second Vatican Council's *Decree on the Church's Missionary Activity (Ad Gentes Divinitus, AGD)*, there is a corresponding grounding of ecclesial mission in the divine missions:

> The pilgrim Church is missionary by her very nature, since it is from the mission of the Son and the mission of the Holy Spirit that she draws her origin, in accordance with the decree of God the Father. (*AGD, #2*)

In theological reflections since the council, there has been a gradually deepening awareness of the interconnection between ecclesial life and divine life. If at the time of the council in the early 1960s the Church as such was the predominant topic of theological reflection, it should also be noted that in the 1980s and 1990s the Trinity has been the subject receiving the most theological attention in the Christian world. Numerous studies of the Trinity have appeared, all of which have argued to some degree or another that the Trinity belongs at the center of Christian life and theological reflection. The *Catechism of the Catholic Church (CCC)* is also very direct about this:

> The mystery of the Most Holy Trinity is the central mystery of Christian faith and life. It is the mystery of God in himself. It is therefore the source of all the other mysteries of faith, the light that enlightens

them. It is the most fundamental and essential teaching in the "hierarchy of the truths of faith"[1]

This refocusing on the Trinity has helped us to recover the genuine center of Christian theology and to situate other theological topics, such as the Church, in their proper context. What is said about the Church, then, is based on what is said about God. This is not to imply that there are no differences between God and the Church with respect to communion and mission. Rather, we are emphasizing that reflection on the Church has as its ultimate reference point our understanding of God.

Unfolding the Vision—The Plan of This Book

This book will develop a vision of the Church according to the rhythm of communion and mission. Of course, much more will need to be said about what these terms mean. What is communion? How do we experience different kinds and degrees of communion with other persons? What is mission? What are the various forms in which it is undertaken? How do Christians of a given time, place, and cultural context embody the call to communion and mission in specific ways of life and activity? We should regularly ask ourselves how we are responding to the mission to make Christian communion more rich, lively, and inclusive.

The following chapters will attempt to spell out the vision. In chapter two we focus on the theme of the Church as a *communion of disciples*. We shall consider in more detail the concept of communion both in terms of the relationships of Christians with God and of Christians with one another. We shall describe the Church as not only a communion of persons but also a communion of disciples. This term will emphasize that our communion with one another does not mean that we are all alike or the same. Rather, the more deeply a person enters into and participates in the communion of the Church, the more profoundly he or she discovers and experiences his or her distinct and indeed unique identity as a person and as a Christian. It is through relationships with others that we come to a deeper knowledge of ourselves. Thus, although all Christians are equal by virtue of Baptism and being created in the image and likeness of God, each of us realizes our Christian identity in a relatively unique way. This chapter will also explore the levels of communion among members of the Church, ranging from the individual household of faith to the local parish community and diocese and ultimately to the universal Church.

In chapter three we take up the ordering or structure of the ecclesial communion. Having established the basic baptismal equality of persons in the Church, how does this community proceed to differentiate among its members in terms of charisms and talents, needs and tasks, ministries and states of life? Some such organization is necessary for the functioning of any community. So in this chapter we shall consider how the diversity of both gifts and tasks in the Church gives rise to different ways of being a Christian. By *states of life* in the Church we are referring to the laity, the ordained, and the consecrated (members of religious communities).

The concept of *orders* in the Church is now used primarily to refer to the various levels of ordained ministry—diaconal (deacons), presbyteral (priests), and episcopal (bishops). The basic meaning of being "ordained" is that a person's relationship to the community as a whole is "ordered" by a particular ministry of service. Historically, though, the term "order" has also been used in a more general way to refer to any distinct class of persons in the Church—such as the order of catechumens, the order of penitents, and the many religious orders. All Christians belong to the "order of the baptized," and on that basis all are called to ministry and mission. Sometimes the Church is described as a *hierarchical communion*, emphasizing the structure given to the Church by the office of ordained ministers, especially the bishops. The perspective of chapter three, while respecting the hierarchical dimension of ecclesial communion, will highlight the presence of gifts for service in all members of the community and the task of orchestrating these gifts for the common good.

In chapter four we reflect on two of the principal means by which the Church is formed as a communion of disciples—the ministries of Word and sacrament. The Church is the gathering of all those who hear the Word of God—the Gospel—and respond to it in faith. Together we continually ponder and unfold the meaning of the Christian message for our lives. According to the Second Vatican Council's *Dogmatic Constitution on Divine Revelation (Dei Verbum, DV)*, "as the centuries succeed one another, the Church constantly moves forward toward the fullness of divine truth, until the words of God reach their complete fulfillment in her" (*DV*, #8). In other words, as history unfolds, the Church is called to continuously deepen its insight into the revealed message of the Gospel, realizing that there is always room for further understanding. We shall see how the entire Church is a learning and teaching community, and how each of us is called to play a role in this ongoing discovery of truth.

At the same time, this community gathered by God's Word expresses and realizes its identity in the most profound way when it celebrates the sacraments. We shall see how the sacraments, above all the Eucharist, "make the Church." Thus, in chapter four we see even more clearly how the entire celebration of Mass—the rite of gathering, the liturgy of the Word, the liturgy of the Eucharist, and the dismissal rite—is the basic experience within which we discover what it is to be Church. In addition we shall explore why the Church itself is called the "sacrament of universal salvation" for the world. This idea of Church as "sacrament for the world" also serves as a transition or bridge to the following chapters, which take up the mission of the Church in the world.

Thus, while in chapters two, three, and four we primarily develop the theme of communion, or the "inner" life of the Church, in chapters five and six we turn our attention to an emphasis on mission, that is, the "outer" life of the Church. In chapter five, we examine the mission of the Church as "evangelizer of cultures." In this perspective all of the ministries and activities of the Church in the world will be understood as part of the process of evangelization. The term "evangelization," somewhat of a newcomer to the Catholic vocabulary, is of central importance for understanding the Church. In his 1975 apostolic exhortation *On Evangelization in the Modern World (Evangelii Nuntiandi, EN)*, Pope Paul VI taught that the task of evangelizing all people constitutes the essential mission of the Church: "Evangelization is in fact the grace and vocation proper to the Church, her deepest identity" (*EN*, #14).

Pope John Paul II has further deepened the Church's identity as an evangelizing community and has emphasized how the evangelization of cultures is always at the same time the "inculturation" of the Gospel.

In chapter six we turn toward a more specific element of the Church's evangelizing activity in the world; namely, transforming human society in the light of the Gospel. Here we consider the role of the Church in the various domains of life in the world, such as the family, the economy, politics, the media, the arts and sciences, and so on. Inspired by the teaching of *GS*, the Church has declared that "action on behalf of justice . . . fully appears to us as a constitutive dimension of preaching the Gospel" (*Justice in the World [JW]*). We shall see how the Church has developed a body of social teaching that inspires us to work for a more justly ordered world. At the same time, Christians, and thus the Church, are called to be in the world but not of the world. Reflection on the Church's social mission will take place with the clear realization that the full scope of that mission extends beyond the things of this world and without the utopian expectation that we can create a perfect society on earth.

Finally, in chapter seven we connect this developed vision of the Church as communion and mission with our profession of belief in the Nicene Creed that the Church is "one, holy, catholic, and apostolic." These traditional marks of the Church have often served as the primary themes for organizing a study of the Church, an ecclesiology. We shall see that by speaking extensively of communion and mission, we do in fact thoroughly study the Church as one and apostolic. Thus, in chapter seven, we offer some further comments on the Church as holy and catholic. These defining attributes of the Church are both gift and task. That is, being one, holy, catholic, and apostolic is both what the Church is as well as what the Church is called to *become*.

Summary

The goal of this book is to inspire a theological vision that incorporates the most important trends in the theology of the Church since the Second Vatican Council. It is my conviction that the rhythm of communion and mission, gathering and being sent— rooted in the very life of God, celebrated in the liturgy, and lived out in the world—provides the only adequate framework for gaining a comprehensive vision of the Church. This is the vision that we seek to put into practice as we journey together in our lives as Christians.

Endnote

1. *CCC* 234: *General Catechetical Directory (GCD)* 47.

For Reflection

1. How would you describe your present "vision" of the Church?

2. Do you experience in your faith community and its liturgy a rhythm of gathering and being sent, coming together and going forth, and communion and mission?

What does it mean to say that the Trinity is the source of the Church's communion and mission?

CHAPTER 2

The Church—Communion of Disciples

We begin this chapter by observing that the Church has both a visible structure or organization as well as invisible bonds connecting its members to one another and to God. These dimensions are often referred to as the *institutional* and the *mystical*. The institutional organization of the Church is reflected in the various offices, structures, and ways of life that establish specific types of relationships among members of the Church, for example, the relationships of pastor to parish, of bishop to diocese, and of local churches to the universal Church. Thus, the Church has a recognizable structure. But the Church is also to be understood from the mystical perspective. The term "mystical" does not refer to the occult or the strange but to the openness, depth, and mystery of relationships among persons. There is among members of the Church a spiritual connection, a sharing of the life of grace, a sharing of life in Christ and in the Spirit.

Both dimensions, the institutional and the mystical, are necessary elements in the life of the Church. Imagine if either were absent. Without the mystical element, relationships in the Church would become merely formal and contractual, with no underlying enthusiasm or spiritual depth. Without the institutional element, the life of the Church would lack the organization and structure within which relationships flourish.

Most associations of persons reflect a similar makeup. For example, in a typical family there are both the visible roles of husband, wife, and children (and other relatives) and the particular bonds of affection—spousal, parental, filial—that represent the spirit or the life of the family. We know that two families may be visibly identical in roles and structure but vastly different in the quality of their common life. Likewise, Catholic parishes typically have very similar organizational structures, yet some parishes are known to be more "alive" than others. Conversely, there may be movements in the Church that falter, not for lack of enthusiasm but for lack of organization. Indeed, in the life of the Church, the institutional and the mystical belong together and can never be separated.

To understand this complex unity of the Church, we follow the approach taken in *Lumen Gentium*, which devotes its first chapter to the mystery of the Church before turning to the institutional structure of the Church and the relations between various types of persons in the Church. This is a very significant arrangement, one that is not accidental. Prior to the Second Vatican Council, most Catholic ecclesiologies focused primarily on the institutional and hierarchical structure of the Church. *LG* meant to correct that one-sided perspective and to establish the fact that what comes first in the Church are the bonds connecting us to God the Father and one another through Christ and in the Spirit. Only secondarily do we relate to one another as persons having different roles and positions.

In other words, for example, a layperson in the Church meets and relates to his or her pastor first as a fellow Christian and secondly as an ordained priest. Of course, there are not really two meetings or relatings, only one; still, it is important to bear this distinction in mind. It may be helpful to recall a passage from one of the sermons of St. Augustine:

> What I am *for* you terrifies me; what I am *with* you consoles me. For you I am a bishop; but with you I am a Christian. The former is a duty, the latter a grace. The former is a danger; the latter, salvation.
>
> (Sermon 340, 1, as cited in
> *LG*, #32, emphasis added)

In this chapter, we focus on the mystical dimension of the Church. We explore what it means to be in spiritual communion with other persons. We indicate how communion is experienced on various levels within the Church. Finally, the term "communion of disciples" is proposed as a particularly good image for expressing our life in the Church.

Communion—Bond of Life in the Church

In the years since the Second Vatican Council, there has been a growing recognition that communion best describes the spiritual bonds that connect Christians to one another and to God in the Church. For example, a synod or meeting of bishops called by John Paul II in 1985 to reflect upon the Second Vatican Council twenty years after its closing observed that

> the ecclesiology of communion is a central and fundamental concept in the conciliar documents. Koinonia-communion, finding its source in Sacred Scripture, was a concept held in great honor in the early Church and in the Oriental Churches, and this teaching endures to the present day. Much was done by the Second Vatican Council to bring about a clearer understanding of the Church as commu-nion and its concrete application to life. What, then, does this complex word "communion" mean? Its fundamental meaning speaks of the union with God brought about by Jesus Christ in the Holy Spirit.
> (Synod of Bishops, Second Extraordinary Assembly Final Report, II, C, #1)

In 1992, the Congregation for the Doctrine of the Faith, one of the departments of the Vatican, issued a short letter entitled "Some Aspects of the Church as Communion," which offered guidance on the interpretation of the concept of communion. This letter notes that

> the concept of communion lies at the heart of the Church's self-understanding, insofar as it is the mystery of the personal union of each human being with the divine Trinity and with the rest of mankind, initiated with the faith and, having begun as a reality in the Church on earth, is directed towards its eschatological fulfillment in the heavenly Church. (#3)

One of the more noteworthy appeals to the ecclesiology of communion comes in the rich reflections of Pope John Paul II in *CL*:

> Again we turn to the words of Jesus: "I am the true vine and my Father is the vinedresser. . . Abide in me and I in you" (John 15:1, 4). These simple words reveal the mystery of communion that serves as the unifying bond between the Lord and his disciples, between Christ and the baptized: a living and life-giving communion through which Christians no longer belong to themselves but are the Lord's very own, as the branches are one with the vine.
>
> The communion of Christians with Jesus has the communion of God as Trinity, namely, the unity of the Son to the Father in the gift of the Holy Spirit, as its model and source, and is itself the means to achieve this communion: united to the Son in the Spirit's bond of love, Christians are united to the Father.
>
> Jesus continues: "I am the vine, you are the branches" (John 15:5). From the communion that Christians experience in Christ there immediately flows the communion which they experience with one another: all are branches of a single vine, namely, Christ. In this communion is the wonderful reflection and participation in the mystery of the intimate life of love in God as Trinity, Father, Son, and Holy Spirit as revealed by the Lord Jesus. . . . Such communion is the very mystery of the Church. (#18)

We have cited these documents at some length to demonstrate the recent prominence of this theme. The *experience* of communion lies at the heart of being the Church; thus, the *concept* of communion lies at the heart of a theology of the Church.

When most of us consider our experience of ecclesial communion we may first think of the fellowship that we have with other members of the faith community. Naturally, this fellowship is shared more deeply with some people than with others; nonetheless, all members of the Church are bonded one to another in some degree. But as the above references make clear, the communion that human persons share among themselves is itself a common sharing in a more basic communion: the communion of persons that is the triune God. If we wish to understand the full significance of communion ecclesiology, then we should approach the subject in three stages: first, the relationship among Father, Son, and Spirit; second, communion among divine persons and human persons; and third, communion among human persons.

Father, Son, and Spirit—A Life of Perfect Communion

What we can know about the life of God is, of course, quite limited and imperfect. Still, as Christians we believe that God has made it possible for us not only to know something about the divine life but to participate in that very life.

The Church confesses its faith in the one God who is Father, Son, and Holy Spirit. This confession, nourished in worship, has from the beginning of the Church's life been the very framework of baptismal, eucharistic, and credal prayers. By the end of the fourth century, the Church came to a consensus regarding the formula of its faith confession about God: one God who is three persons. In our attempts to gain some understanding of this great mystery, the Christian tradition has pondered what it means for God to be three persons. Such reflection is in turn crucial for us to understand what it means to be human persons, if we take seriously the teaching of Genesis that God created men and women in the divine image (see Genesis 1:27).

The most important insight about the meaning of personhood is that we only truly become persons in and through our relationships with others. We come to our identity as persons when we make a gift of ourselves to others and, reciprocally, receive in ourselves the gifts of others. We discover what it is to be a human person through this rhythm of giving and receiving precisely because this very rhythm is first of all characteristic of God's life. The Father, Son, and Holy Spirit are who they are because they share a life of complete giving and receiving. The Father gives everything he is to the Son; in turn, the Son receives all that he is from the Father. But this bond of love is totally mutual and equal; therefore, we also believe that the Son gives everything he is back to the Father, who receives the Son's complete love. So profound is this mutual love that it exists also as a person, whom we confess to be the Holy Spirit.

All of this may sound quite abstract, but the basic point is utterly crucial: We become human persons, and not just isolated individuals, insofar as we enter into the pattern of self-giving and receiving that is first God's life. And it is this self-giving and receiving that creates communion, a communion of persons. Of course, we must continuously discern how we are called to make these general principles concrete and actual in our own lives. How are we to give ourselves away to others? And how do we come to be who we are through the gifts of others?

We Are Invited to Share God's Life

Christians confess that in sending the Son and the Holy Spirit into the world, God the Father offers us the opportunity to participate in the divine life of communion. Here is how the Second Vatican Council's document on divine revelation, *DV*, puts it:

> In His goodness and wisdom God chose to reveal Himself and to make known to us the hidden purpose of his will (see Eph.1:9) by which through Christ, the Word made flesh, man might in the Holy Spirit have access to the Father and come to share in the divine nature (see Eph. 2:18; 2 Peter 1:4). Through this revelation, therefore, the invisible God (see Col.1:15; 1 Tim. 1:17) out of the abundance of

His love speaks to men as friends (see Ex. 33:11; John 15:14–15) and lives among them (see Bar. 3:38), so that He may invite and take them into fellowship with Himself. (#2)

This rich passage distills the essential message of the Gospel: God comes to us in Word and Spirit that we may share the fullness of God's life. The witness of the New Testament and the Christian tradition is that a new kind of life has been made available to us, a kind of life that is distinct from (though not separate from) the biological and natural life we experience as humans.

Many images and terms have been used to describe this newness of life: being born again, or created anew, being saved, redeemed, reconciled, made God-like, and so on. Our experience of this new life clearly involves a change in us, a change we call conversion. And in the experience of conversion, as in any change, there is both a *what* and a *how*, that is, the process of change involves both what we become and how we get there.

Jesus and the Spirit correspond to the what and how of conversion. Our conversion involves becoming more and more like Jesus, becoming more and more the kind of person he is, a person who makes a gift of self to others and in turn receives their gifts. So the New Testament speaks of our being transformed into his likeness, his image, his "form" (for example, see Romans 8:29, 2 Corinthians 3:18). But how does this conversion take place? What causes it to happen? Is it simply a matter of our own effort and striving? The message of the New Testament is that the prime mover in this process is the Holy Spirit, working from within us. So the Holy Spirit is described as being "poured into our hearts" (Romans 5:5) or "sent . . . into our hearts" (Galatians 4:6). The work of the Holy Spirit is, quite simply, to transform us into the likeness of Christ. And because Christ is both fully human and fully divine, this transformation makes us at once more human and gives us a share in the divine nature. Finally, the result of the process leads us back to God the Father, in that we become adopted sons or daughters, saying with Jesus, our brother, "Abba, Father" (see Galatians 4:4–6).

So the divine communion of persons is acting to change us, to transform us, and thereby to draw us into their own company. In the process, each of us is brought into a bond with Christ, incorporated into Christ, into the body of Christ. In the words of *LG*:

> By communicating His Spirit, Christ made His brothers [and sisters], called together from all nations, mystically the components of His own Body. In that body the life of Christ is poured into the believers who, through the sacraments, are united in a hidden and real way to Christ who suffered and was glorified. (#7)

The image of the vine and the branches, taken from the Gospel of John, is, as we saw above, another metaphor for referring to the unifying bond between Christ and his followers. But as was indicated by John Paul, "From the communion that Christians experience in Christ there immediately flows the communion which they experience with one another" (*CL*, #18). And so we now consider the experience of communion among the members of the Church.

Communion Among Members of the Church

What connects Christians to one another is their common participation in the divine life: the indwelling of the one Spirit in each member, the incorporation of each member into the one Christ, the common status as an adopted son or daughter of the one Father. Further, members of the Church share in the *means* by which these relationships are actualized, sustained, and furthered, especially the preaching of the Gospel, the sacraments, and the various ministries within the Church. The original meaning of the term "communion of saints" derives from the sharing of the holy things of God among the people of the Church.

But communion among Christians is also reflected in the sharing of everything, spiritual and material, that is good about our life. This sharing of goods is never generic or abstract; we always share and exchange specific goods with particular persons. The Church is not simply one large communion of persons, though there are real bonds connecting every member of the Church with every other member. It is more accurate to say that the Church is a "communion of communions." To accurately describe the richness of ecclesial communion requires us to take account of various types of "ecclesial units," that is, associations of Christians. A household, a parish, a diocese, and the universal Church are all examples of ecclesial units.

In the vision proposed here, the parish may be thought of as a communion of households; the diocese may be thought of as a communion of parishes; and the universal Church may be thought of as a communion of dioceses. *Lumen Gentium* speaks explicitly about the relationship between the universal Church and the "particular" or "local" church, which in this context means the diocesan church. In paragraph 23, *LG* recognizes the particular churches as "fashioned after the model of the universal Church, in and from which churches comes into being the one and only Catholic Church." The idea of the universal Church as a communion of local churches has subsequently become quite common. It seems legitimate to extend the idea to the diocesan and parochial levels as well.

The Parish—Communion of Households

The most basic ecclesial unit is the household of faith. In the New Testament period and for some time thereafter, Christians assembled in one another's homes for worship and fellowship because their numbers were small and there were no public spaces available for them in which to safely congregate. These early communities were known as "house churches." In our use of the term "household of faith," we are not referring to a house church in this sense, although there is some resonance with this earlier experience in the history of the Church. Rather, we take our inspiration from the concept of the "domestic church," which appears in *LG* (#11) and in other documents.

LG speaks of the domestic Church—the typical household of an individual nuclear family composed of parents and children—and stresses the catechetical responsibility of the parents to the children. Parents are the "first preachers of the faith" (#11), or the first teachers of the faith for their children. The family unit is the basic cell of both society and the Church, and is itself an instance of a communion of persons.

Not every household, however, is a family in the sense in which official Church documents speak. Households may be made up of single persons, or of unrelated adults living together, for example. Other households include multiple generations of family living together. Some households, then, are more specifically themselves a communion of persons than are others, but all households in which members of the Church live are called to be places where faith is nurtured and sustained. The term "household of faith," then, is intended to be a broad and inclusive interpretation of the term "domestic church."

For most members of the Church, the bonds of communion are experienced and lived out most regularly at the household and parish level. The parish is not only a communion of households but also a communion of other ecclesial associations and movements that may be more or less numerous depending on the parish. Some parishes may have groupings of neighborhood churches or small faith communities, in which a small cluster of households regularly comes together for prayer, fellowship, study, and mutual support. Other subgroupings in the parish also represent opportunities for more intense interpersonal exchange and relationship, for example, youth groups, choirs, those involved in the parish school, participants in movements such as Cursillo or Marriage Encounter, and members of organizations such as the Knights of Columbus or the St. Vincent de Paul Society.

In such ways as these, the parish community provides numerous opportunities for its members to experience communion with one another. And what, again, is the heart of the experience of ecclesial communion? It is the mutual exchange of our material and spiritual goods and talents, and of our very selves for the building up of the Church in a given time and place. It is the experience of interpersonal presence, dialogue, and conversation through which we manifest ourselves to one another and grow in the sharing of our lives as Christians. In sum, communion occurs to the extent that we make a gift of ourselves to others and correspondingly receive from others the gifts that they offer.

Thus, ideally, the diverse charisms and talents of the people of God are communicated to one another. So one person's gift of humor brings joy to others in need of uplifting. One person's gift for organization can make a successful parish social possible. The gifts of those with musical talent make the liturgy lively and spirited. Personal characteristics, professional competencies, resources of financial and material goods—all of these are blessings of which we are stewards, blessings available for the building up of communion. The diversity of charisms and treasures in a community is the basis for the variety of ministries in that community.

The Diocese—Communion of Parishes

In the same way that the parish is a communion of households, so the diocese is a communion of parishes. Just as the pastor of the parish is the person with primary responsibility for overseeing the unity of the parish, so the bishop is the person with primary responsibility for overseeing the unity of the diocese. In fact, the meaning of the word *bishop* literally is "overseer" in the original Greek. Individuals and households, of course, participate in activities at the diocesan and parochial level. But in addition, parish communities as such may also engage in a mutual exchange of gifts that fosters further levels of communion.

Such an exchange between local Christian communities is attested to in the earliest New Testament period. Paul speaks at various points of the collections taken up from all the churches he had founded, on behalf of the poorer churches of Judea. For example, to the Romans he says:

> At present, however, I am going to Jerusalem in a ministry to the saints; for Macedonia and Achaia have been pleased to share their resources with the poor among the saints at Jerusalem. They were pleased to do this, and indeed they owe it to them; for if the Gentiles have come to share in their spiritual blessings, they ought also to be of service to them in material things. (15:25–27)

This mutual sharing (Paul uses the term *koinonia*) between the communities helped to strengthen the bonds of communion among them. Of course, this example predates the establishment of the diocesan structure of the Church, but the point is that today, just as then, there is a real communion that exists between faith communities as such. Sometimes this takes on more tangible expressions, such as when a relatively affluent suburban parish adopts a poorer inner-city or rural parish as a "sister" parish. Or again, several parishes may jointly support a parochial school. More typically, this level of communion is realized in the common support of the parishes for diocesan programs and activities.

The Universal Church—Communion of Local Churches

Part of the recovery of the ecclesiology of communion at the Second Vatican Council involved a renewed vision of the relationship between local (diocesan) churches and the universal Church. Pre-conciliar ecclesiology had tended to give the impression that local or particular churches were simply parts or branches of the one universal Church and that only in the universal Church as such could the true Church of Christ be found. This perspective grew out of a strong tendency in the nineteenth and early twentieth centuries to centralize authority in the Roman Catholic Church in the office of the papacy and the central administration of the Church in Rome.

We have already noted that *LG* states that the particular churches are "fashioned after the model of the universal Church" and that from such churches "comes into being the one and only Catholic Church" (#23). That document goes on to teach that

> This Church of Christ is truly present in all legitimate local congregations of the faithful which, united with their pastors, are also called churches in the New Testament. . . . In these communities, though frequently small and poor, or living in the Diaspora, Christ is present, and in virtue of His presence there is brought together one, holy, catholic and apostolic Church. (#26)

This teaching should not be interpreted to mean that the universal Church is simply the sum of all the local churches. Rather, it is more sound to say that the universal Church and the local churches come into existence simultaneously. The first community of Christians at Pentecost was at the same time the one universal Church of Christ and the local church of Jerusalem. As communities of Christians (churches) were established elsewhere, Christ's Church was still one, but that one universal Church was now actualized in a diversity of local churches. Each local church, so to say, is wholly the Church, although it is not the whole Church.

The one universal Catholic Church is thus a communion of local churches. Therefore, relations among the local churches are marked by the same kind of mutual exchange of gifts that we have observed at smaller levels of groupings. Just as pastors and bishops have the particular responsibility of serving the unity of parishes and dioceses, the specific ministry of the bishop of Rome, the pope, is to maintain and preserve the communion of the diverse local churches of the world.

LG also considered the relations between the Roman Catholic Church and other Christian churches from the perspective of an ecclesiology of communion. *LG* did not identify, as earlier documents had, the mystical body of Christ with the visible Roman Catholic Church; rather, it stated that the one Church of Christ "subsists" in the Catholic Church (#8). This statement and references in the council's *Decree on Ecumenism (Unitatis Redintegratio, UR)* maintain a distinction between "the one Church of Christ" and the "Catholic Church." The council teaches that the fullness of the means for achieving communion—the ministries of Word, sacrament, and pastoral leadership—are found only in the Catholic Church. Other Christian communities, however, possess many of the elements proper to the Church of Christ, such as the preaching of the Gospel, some degree of sacramental life, gifts of the Holy Spirit, and a community of faith. This allows us to say that the one Church of Christ, as a communion of churches, would include, in a real though less than complete way, the Orthodox churches and the churches of the Reformation.

Communion Beyond the Visible Church

So deep and strong are the bonds that join Christians together that not even death undoes them. The doctrine of the communion of saints expresses the conviction that the pilgrim Church, the community of Christians on earth, is united with those Christians who have passed from this life. Again, to cite *LG*:

> Therefore the union of the wayfarers with the brethren who have gone to sleep in the peace of Christ is not in the least weakened or interrupted, but on the contrary, according to the perpetual faith of the Church, is strengthened by communication of spiritual goods. (#49)

The spiritual goods exchanged here are in the form of prayers: the prayers of the earthly Church for the dead and the intercession of the saints in heaven for those here on earth. While we may be inclined to limit the saints in the term "communion of saints" to the relatively few canonized saints, the New Testament sense of the term refers to all members of the Christian community. To be a saint is the destiny of every Christian (indeed, of every human being), a destiny that at least should have its beginnings in our present experience.

In principle, the Church is intended to be a totally comprehensive communion of every human being who has ever lived and who will live in the future. The Church is a sign of the communion that God wills for his entire people. The large majority of people, in fact, have not lived on earth within the visible Christian community, much less the Roman Catholic Church. And yet the impulse, the mission, of the Church must be toward the inclusion of every human being within its communion. We can and must hope that this will be realized in the complete fulfillment of God's plan for humanity.

The Church—Communion of Disciples

We bring this chapter to a conclusion with some remarks on the Church as the communion of disciples. While no single phrase or term or image can completely capture everything that needs to be said about the Church, this phrase does serve in a compact way to pull together much of what has been said in this chapter and to prepare for what follows.

Why the term "communion of disciples"? The term "disciple," which literally means "learner," is prominent in the New Testament and refers to the followers of Jesus. It is a term that recommends itself for a number of reasons. First, "disciple" is a term that refers to every Christian equally, prior to and going beyond one's specific role in the Church. Some theologians have utilized the phrase "discipleship of equals" to emphasize that, in the Church, who we are in common is more important than who we are in particular positions, even in positions of high authority.

Second, the term underscores the fact that all Christians are learners, indeed, all members of the Church are truly beginners in the Christian life. Third, though every Christian is called to be a disciple, each is called in a uniquely personal way. Here is how Pope John Paul II put it in his first encyclical letter, *The Redeemer of Man (Redemptor Hominis, RH)*:

> For the whole of the community of the People of God and for each member of it what is in question is not just a specific "social membership"; rather, for each and every one what is essential is a particular "vocation.". . . Therefore, if we wish to keep in mind this community of the People of God, which is so vast and so extremely differentiated, we must see first and foremost Christ saying in a way to each member of the community: "Follow me." It is the community of the disciples, each of whom in a different way—at times very consciously and consistently, at other times not very consciously and very inconsistently—is following Christ. (#21)

The concept of disciple emphasizes the dignity and value of every single member of the Church, as well as his or her unique personality, charisms, and giftedness by the Spirit. The phrase "communion of disciples" thus balances and expresses the dynamic relationship of unity and diversity, the social and the personal, in the Church. Unity and diversity are not in conflict or contradiction. Rather, precisely the opposite is the case. The greater the depth of communion among disciples, the more the distinct dignity and unique personality of each disciple stands out. And this is how things are in the life of God. The unity of the three divine persons is matched by the distinctive uniqueness of each.

Summary

We are now in a position to move forward and consider the visible structure of the ecclesial communion. The fact that every disciple brings distinct gifts to the community, coupled with the diversity of needs and tasks in the community, establishes the basis from which different ministries, offices, and ways of life arise and interrelate in the Church.

For Reflection

1. How would you describe your experience of communion in the Church? How could you contribute to an enrichment of communion in your faith community?

2. Explore your experience of belonging to the Church at various levels—household, parish, diocese, and universal Church.

3. What is the particular way that Christ is calling you to be a disciple (who will be in communion with other disciples)?

CHAPTER 3

Charisms, Ministries, and States of Life in the Church

aving discussed the spiritual bonds uniting Christians with the triune God and one another, we now turn our attention to the distinct and specific roles, offices, and positions into which the Church is visibly organized. But it should not be thought that spiritual communion comes about prior to or apart from the visible structure of the Church. The variety of gifts, offices, conditions, and ways of life in which members of the Church live not only expresses their communion with one another and God but also constitutes or brings about communion in the Church. The diverse forms of life and activity in the Church are indispensable means through which true communion is achieved. *Lumen Gentium* emphasizes the unity of the mystical and the institutional elements of the Church in this way:

> The society structured with hierarchical organs and the mystical body of Christ, the visible society and the spiritual community, the earthly Church and the Church endowed with heavenly riches, are not to be thought of as two realities. On the contrary, they form one complex reality which comes together from a human and a divine element. (#8)

At the same time, there is a legitimate distinction (not separation) between the life of spiritual communion and the means through which that life is brought about and realized. The means by which communion is brought about—principally, the preaching of the Gospel, the celebration of the sacraments, and pastoral leadership in the Church—exist only to build up that life of communion that is shared by members of the Church. In the life of the world to come, when God's plan for us is completely fulfilled, there will be no preaching, no sacraments, no ecclesial offices. The need for these things will have passed away. Even now, then, their status is somewhat provisional. In the words of Pope John Paul II, "Although the Church possesses a 'hierarchical' structure, nevertheless, this structure is totally ordered to the holiness of Christ's members" *(On the Dignity and Vocation of Women [Mulieris Dignitatem, MD], #27).*

Our starting point in this chapter will be those things that are common to all members of the Church. From there we will see how the distinction of disciples into diverse ways of life and positions takes place, with every difference being ordered to the unity, the communion, of the whole. We will ask about the distinct character of lay, ordained, and religious life in the Church, and we will describe the specialized ministries of priest, bishop, and pope. This discussion will involve a consideration of both the Church's inner life and its mission in the world, which, again, are realities that can be distinguished though never separated.

The Common Status of the People of God

In *LG* the term "People of God" is used in a special way to refer to everything that applies equally to any member of the Church, whether lay, clerical, or religiously professed. This term, one of several images of the Church, seems to be used in subsequent documents in a similar manner, that is, when a document wishes to speak to what pertains to all members of the Church without distinction. We might also point out here that "People of God," while used in these documents to refer to the Church, is also a term that brings to mind the fact that God's ultimate goal is to bring all people into unity as his own.

The first quality that the People of God hold in common is the relationship of each one with Christ. By means of that relationship, each Christian is brought into a participation in the mission and ministry of Christ. He sought to fulfill his one mission, reconciling the world with God his Father, through a variety of ministries, such as teaching, preaching, and healing the sick. One traditional way of summarizing or expressing the ministry of Jesus is to understand Jesus under the titles of "priest," "prophet," and "king." Correspondingly, the People of God, who are at the same time Christ's people, the Body of Christ, are considered a "priestly, prophetic, and royal people." According to the *CCC*:

Jesus Christ is the one whom the Father anointed with the Holy Spirit and established as priest, prophet, and king. The whole People of God participates in these three offices of Christ and bears the responsibilities for mission and service that flow from them. (#783)

These categories, which find their origin in the experience of the Jewish religious tradition in which Jesus was formed, do reflect different aspects of the identity and ministry of Jesus. Still, we may have some difficulty today in understanding the entire range of Christian ministry within these three categories. For example, under which office does catechesis fall? or the ministry of spiritual direction? or youth ministry? Some of the difficulty, of course, lies in our different cultural situation from that of biblical times. For example, because we are no longer governed by kings, what does it mean to us for Jesus to be king and for us to be a royal people? Such questions notwithstanding, documents such as *LG* and the *CCC* continue to employ these categories, and so we need to be aware of how they are being used.

The second common quality of God's people to be considered here is that we have all received gifts from the Holy Spirit. The role of the Holy Spirit is equal to but distinct from that of Christ. While Christ carried out a visible ministry on earth, the Spirit operates from within us, invisibly, as it were. Specifically, the Spirit gifts each of us with a distinct set of personal qualities, characteristics, and talents of which we are stewards. This is a theme that St. Paul reflected on at length. Here is how he puts the matter to the Church at Corinth:

> *Now there are varieties of gifts, but the same Spirit; and there are varieties of service, but the same Lord; and there are varieties of activities, but it is the same God who activates all of them in everyone. To each is given the manifestation of the Spirit for the common good. To one is given through the Spirit the utterance of wisdom, and to another the utterance of knowledge according to the same*

Spirit, to another faith by the same Spirit, to another gifts of healing by the one Spirit, to another the working of miracles, to another prophecy, to another the discernment of spirits, to another various kinds of tongues, to another the interpretation of tongues. All these are activated by one and the same Spirit, who allots to each one individually just as the Spirit chooses.

(1 Corinthians 12:4–11)

Several points are to be observed in understanding the gifts of the Holy Spirit. First, Paul's word for "gift" is *charisma*, which we also translate as "charism." The word "charism" is the common theological term for referring to a gift given by the Holy Spirit. Second, charisms are given not for personal aggrandizement but for service *(diakonia)* to the communion *(koinonia)* of the Church. Third, we should consider any good quality or virtue or talent as a charism of the Holy Spirit. Being a good listener is a charism of the Holy Spirit; so is having a gift for administration, for consoling the grieving, for being a good parent, for resolving conflicts. The word should not be narrowly restricted to refer to so-called extraordinary or spectacular gifts of the Holy Spirit. Likewise, its meaning should not be confined to obviously religious or "churchy" qualities. Fourth, we have an ongoing responsibility to develop the charisms that we have been given. And at different points in our lives, given our changing circumstances and experiences, we may expect to discover new charisms. It is generally the case, as well, that the discovery and identification of charisms comes about not so much by our own self-reflection but through the feedback that we receive from other persons.

Our shared call to participate in Christ's ministry and our endowment with charisms by the Holy Spirit are to be matched to the various needs and tasks that are required for the Church both to realize its life of communion and to carry out its mission in the world. Some of these needs are of a kind that any community would have, for example, the need for leadership and the exercise of authority. Other needs are more specific to the Christian community in its taking up of the mission and ministry of Christ, such as preaching the Word of God. These needs are obviously numerous and wide-ranging, given everything that the Church is and does. The diversity of ecclesial tasks is witnessed to at several points in the New Testament; here is a passage from the Letter to the Ephesians:

> Each of us was given grace according to the measure of Christ's gift. . . . The gifts he gave were that some would be apostles, some prophets, some evangelists, some pastors and teachers, to equip the saints for the work of ministry, for building up the body of Christ.
> (4:7,11–12; see also 1 Corinthians 12:28; Romans 12:4–8)

Ecclesial tasks, such as teaching and pastoring, are ongoing responsibilities of the Christian community. As such there arises the need for and existence of a diversity of ecclesial offices, that is, relatively stable institutional positions through which persons carry out ministries to serve the mission of the Church, which is the mission of Christ himself. In the Catholic Church there is a particular structure of such offices that is of prime importance for understanding the Church, namely, the ordained offices of bishop, priest, and deacon. We will have more to say about these particular offices later in this chapter.

The Church Evolves Through History

Our next step is to establish the proper correspondence among charisms, tasks, and offices in the Church. To do so we must consider how the Church came into existence historically, as well as its evolution from the very earliest New Testament communities up to the present time.

When does the Church actually begin to come into existence? There is not a simple answer to this question. According to *LG*, the Church comes into existence, as it were, by degrees or stages. "Already from the beginning of the world the foreshadowing of the Church took place" (#2), and the community of the Israelites in the Old Testament in some sense "was already called the Church of God" (#9). With the coming of Jesus into the world, the Church appears in ever-greater degrees of realization. In his public ministry and in the gathering of his first disciples, Jesus "set it [the Church] on its course by preaching the Good News, that is, the coming of the kingdom of God" (#5). And, in an image beloved by the Church fathers, "This inauguration and this growth [of the Church] are both symbolized by the blood and water which flowed from the open side of a crucified Jesus" (#3; see John 19:34). After his resurrection, Christ "poured out on his disciples the Spirit promised by the Father"; the Church henceforth "receives the mission to proclaim and to spread among all peoples the Kingdom of Christ and of God and to be, on earth, the initial budding forth of that kingdom" (#5). Finally,

> At the end of time it will gloriously achieve completion, when, as is read in the Fathers, all the just from Adam and "from Abel, the just one, to the last of the elect" will be gathered together with the Father in the universal Church. (#2)

It seems, then, that the Church must be thought of as a historically evolving community. It assumes different forms at various moments in history. But the overarching destiny of the Church, that to which it continually tends, is the communion of all people with the triune God. This goal is what has theological priority in our ecclesiology, our understanding of the Church. Office and structure exist to serve that communion and to promote the holiness of its members. *LG* affirms this point of view by placing chapters on "The Mystery of the Church" and "The People of God" before chapters dealing with the distinction of God's people according to different offices and states of life. Indeed, "everything that has been said. . . concerning the People of God is intended for the laity, religious and clergy alike" (#30).

At a certain point in its history, though, the Church begins to exist as the visible society of the disciples of Jesus with the mission of proclaiming the Gospel in the world and bringing about

the kingdom of God. It is at Pentecost, with the public outpour-
ing of the Holy Spirit on the disciples, that the Church assumes
this form, explicitly taking up the mission and ministry of Christ.
It is from this point on that we must ask the question about the
relation of charism, task, and office in the Church.

The Correspondence of Charisms, Tasks, and Offices

What comes first in the Church is the simultaneous existence of
various tasks or ministries to be performed and persons gifted by the
Spirit with the charism(s) for carrying out those tasks. Ideally, of
course, there is a close correspondence or match between charisms
and tasks. Out of this situation there eventually evolves a more stable structure of offices, although the emergence of charisms also
continues as the Church grows, develops, and encounters new situations with corresponding new tasks.

The primary tasks to be carried out in the Church after
Pentecost were the proclamation of the Gospel and the founding
of new communities of Christians. Those who performed these
activities were known as apostles. So *apostle* ("one who is sent")
was a specific role in which certain persons carried out crucial
ecclesial ministries.

Who were the apostles? The New Testament tells us that the
necessary criteria for being an apostle were (1) witnessing an
appearance of the risen Christ and (2) receiving from the risen
Christ the commission to preach the Gospel in an authoritative
manner. On this basis apostles founded churches in both Jewish
and Gentile contexts. It should be noted that "the apostles" are
not identical with "the Twelve." The apostles were a wider group
than the Twelve and included Paul; James the brother of the
Lord; and Barnabas. Apostles, including the Twelve, were themselves chosen from an already existing community of disciples of
Jesus. It is clear, for example, that when the need arose to replace
Judas Iscariot among the Twelve, a choice was made from among

those "who have accompanied us during all the time that the Lord Jesus went in and out among us" (Acts 1:21).

Furthermore, though there is a transmission of leadership in which apostles are eventually succeeded by bishops, strictly speaking, the role of apostle is not transferable. That is, only those who witnessed the risen Lord are eligible to be apostles. From this point of view, "apostle" is not an office that one can succeed to in the Church. Rather, it is a unique role that was filled by a select group of witnesses to the resurrection of Christ, who themselves received charisms of the Holy Spirit for their ministry (see Acts 1:8, 2:4, John 20:22–23).

Thus, from the very beginning of the Church as a public body carrying out the mission and ministry of Christ, there is a process in which the interplay of ecclesial tasks and persons with charisms gives rise to specific roles within the community of disciples. This is the pattern that we find also in the earliest New Testament churches, especially those founded by the apostle Paul. In the New Testament churches we see a plurality of ways of organizing ministries and coordinating tasks and roles. In a relatively short period of time, though, a more stable and consistent structure of official positions began to develop within the various churches. In time this structure came to predominate as a primary way for organizing ecclesial life.

Specifically, a threefold set of offices developed in the early churches. First, there is the *episkopos*, or overseer, of a given community, the person responsible for leadership and authority. This is the office we now refer to as bishop. In a local church, there is only one *episkopos*, one final authority and head of the community. Second, there is the *presbyteros*, the elder, who shared responsibilities for leadership. Typically there was a council of elders in a community. This eventually became the office we refer to as priest. Third, there is the *diakonos*, the deacon, one who assists the overseers and elders in the carrying out of their ministries. This office became that which we today refer to as deacon.

We shall have more to say below about the exercise of episcopal, presbyteral, and diaconal offices and ministries in the

Church. This fundamental form of ecclesial organization, which continues today, is held by the Catholic Church to have come about through the will of God as a divinely intended means for structuring ecclesial life. At the same time, this structure does not exhaust what goes on in the Church in terms of charisms and ministries. Indeed, those who hold these offices have a particular responsibility for cultivating charisms and ministries in the community as a whole. The ritual of ordination symbolizes the importance of these offices and their ministries.

These offices arise in the Church because of the prior presence and correspondence of ecclesial tasks and charisms of the Holy Spirit. There are not two separate classes of persons in the Church, the ordained (the clerical) and the non-ordained (the lay). We do, of course, distinguish between these groups but only from the perspective of a prior and more fundamental unity. All are gifted in the Church; all are called to participate in the mission of Christ by taking up various activities and ministries. So in his reflections on the vocation and mission of the laity, Pope John Paul remarks that

> the Spirit of the Lord gives a vast variety of charisms, inviting people to assume different ministries and forms of service and reminding them, as he reminds all people in their relationship in the Church, that what distinguishes persons is *not an increase in dignity, but a special and complementary capacity for service.*
>
> (*CL*, #20, emphasis added)

States of Life in the Church—Laity, Clergy, and Religious

The presence and exercise of the variety of charisms and ministries and the development of an institutional structure of offices gives rise to what have traditionally been called the different "states of life" in the Church. These are the laity, the clergy (ordained ministers), and those who have professed vows in a religious order. We shall briefly discuss each of these in turn, focusing upon the specific "character" of each. First, however, we take note of the prior unity and coordination among the various states. Again, we turn to remarks by Pope John Paul II:

All the members of the People of God—clergy, men and women religious, the lay faithful—are laborers in the vineyard. At one and the same time they all are the goal and subjects of Church communion as well as of participation in the mission of salvation. Every one of us possessing charisms and ministries, diverse yet complementary, works in the one and the same vineyard of the Lord. . . .

In Church communion the states of life, by being ordered one to the other, are thus bound together among themselves. They all share in a deeply basic meaning: that of being *the manner of living out the commonly shared Christian dignity and the universal call to holiness in the perfection of love*. They are *different yet complementary*, in the sense that each of them has a basic and unmistakable character which sets each apart, while at the same time each of them is seen in relation to the other and placed at each other's service.

Thus the lay state of life has its distinctive feature in its secular character. It fulfills an ecclesial service in bearing witness and, in its own way recalling for priests, women and men religious, the significance of the earthly and temporal realities in the salvific plan of God. In turn, the *ministerial* priesthood represents in different times and places, the permanent guarantee of the sacramental presence of Christ the Redeemer. The religious state bears witness to the eschatological character of the

Church, that is, the straining towards the Kingdom of God that is prefigured and in some way anticipated and experienced even now through the vows of chastity, poverty and obedience.

All the states of life, whether taken collectively or individually in relation to the others, are at the service of the Church's growth. While different in expression they are deeply united in the Church's "mystery of communion" and are dynamically coordinated in its unique mission.

(*CL*, #55, emphasis added)

What comes across emphatically in this passage is the equal participation in ecclesial communion and mission of all the diverse members of the Church. The existence of diverse states of life does not create different classes of persons or divisions according to status. There is a recognition, though, that no one is a Christian or a member of the Church in a generic sense. Concretely, a person is stamped with the particular character of a given form of life. We turn now to a brief consideration of the character of each state of life.

THE LAY STATE—RENEWING THE WHOLE TEMPORAL ORDER

All persons in the Church belong originally to the laity. Some take up more specialized roles at some point, but the majority find their vocations as part of the lay faithful. As the distinction of lay, clerical, and religious life emerged in the history of the Church, there has been a struggle to understand what exactly is the distinctive quality of the lay vocation. Often the laity have been defined by what they are not—ordained, consecrated. Recently, a more positive account has been offered: The laity have a "secular character," which obliges them to work toward the "Christian animation of the temporal order." Some clarification of these terms is now called for.

The word "secular" here simply means, "pertaining to the world, the affairs of the world." While at times in the history of Christianity, a sharp division, even a separation, of the "secular" from the "sacred" has been proposed, the deepest instinct of Christians is to understand the created world as the place in which God is present and active. Christianity is, after all, a religion in which God becomes incarnate, that is, becomes human in this world. The world, then, is a religious reality and should not be thought of otherwise.

The phrase "temporal order" refers to all those affairs that make up human activity in time, in history, in this world. This would include politics, the economy, the arts and sciences, family life, and other regions of social and cultural life. "Temporal order" may be compared to "eternal order" in the same way that "secular" is compared to "sacred"—by way of distinction, not separation. So Christians are called to be in the world but not of the world. Thus we do maintain a legitimate distinction between the secular and the sacred, the temporal order and the eternal order. Christians should not spend their time in this world as if they really lived somewhere else but neither should they give the impression that they live in this world as if they would always remain in it.

Lay Christians, then, are called to participate in Christ's mission and ministry especially by their lives in the secular affairs described above. This does not exclude lay Christians from specifically "churchly" ministries, but it does point to their special charisms. Their mission is to infuse the values of the Gospel into all realms of life on earth—the political, the economic, the domestic, the artistic, the scientific, the commercial, the legal, and so on. This does not mean, however, that we are obliged to establish explicitly Christian governments and institutions but that in our personal and professional lives we bring the spirit of the Gospel to whatever we do. We shall have much more to say about this form of the Church's mission in chapter six.

We must emphasize that to regard the character of the lay state as pertaining to the secular does not create a dualism between the secular and the sacred, or between laity and clergy, or between the world and the Church. All of creation is graced, and God is just as much present in the ordinary experiences of life as in those that are explicitly religious. The Church is a sign, a sacrament, that makes manifest and brings to explicit expression what is implicitly present in all of creation—God's gracious offer of communion.

WHAT IS LAY MINISTRY?

Although the primary vocation of the lay faithful is in the world, lay members of the Church are also very involved in many activities that pertain more directly to the inner life of the Church itself. Thus we refer to ecclesial lay ministries, such as being a catechist, a member of the liturgy planning team, or a member of the parish council. In a typical parish, lay people are involved in many such ministries. But here we come up against a question: What, exactly, is lay ministry?

To address this question, it is important to recall that, for most of the history of the Church (though not the earliest period nor most recently), the term "ministry" referred exclusively to the activity of the ordained. Thus, for example, the distinction is regularly made between the "ministerial priesthood" (of the ordained) and the "common priesthood" (the participation of all the baptized in the priestly office of Christ). As stated in *LG*:

> Though they differ from one another in essence and not only in degree, the common priesthood of the faithful and the ministerial or hierarchical priesthood are nonetheless interrelated; each of them in its own special way is a participation in the one priesthood of Christ. (#10)

The impression is given here and at some points in other official documents that the priestly, prophetic, and royal activity of the non-ordained cannot properly be referred to as ministry. But it is so referred to at other points in *LG* and in other documents; further, since the Second Vatican Council, it has become common in the Church to refer, for example, to lay ministries of many different kinds. It is clear that we are not going to stop describing these activities of the laity as ministries.

Still, there persists an ambivalence, at least in official documents, about the use of the term "ministry." A document entitled "On Certain Questions Regarding the Collaboration of the Non-Ordained Faithful in the Sacred Ministry of Priest," released by the Vatican in 1997, was extremely cautious about referring to the activity of the non-ordained as ministry:

> In some cases the extension of the term "ministry" to the *munera* [tasks] belonging to the lay faithful has been permitted by the fact that the latter, to their own degree, are a participation in the one priesthood of Christ. The *officia* [offices] temporarily entrusted to them, however, are exclusively the result of a deputation by the Church. . . .
>
> In this original sense the term *ministry (servitium)* expresses only the work by which the Church's members continue the mission and ministry of Christ within her and the whole world. However, when the term is distinguished from and compared with the various *munera* and *officia*, then it should be clearly noted that *only* in virtue of sacred ordination does the work obtain that full, univocal meaning that tradition has attributed to it.
>
> The non-ordained faithful may be generically designated "extraordinary ministers" when deputed by competent authorities to discharge, solely by way of supply, those offices mentioned in Canon 230, p. 3, and in Canons 943 and 1112. Naturally, the concrete term may be applied to those to whom functions are canonically entrusted, e.g., catechists, acolytes, lectors, etc.
>
> (Article 1, #2, 3)

How are we to understand this passage? Its overarching goal, which is quite legitimate, is to preserve the distinct character of ordained ministry. In attempting to do so, however, the text unfortunately seems to question whether any activity of the non-ordained can *properly* be referred to as ministry. What must be understood is that some activities and offices (e.g., lector, eucharistic minister, minister of Baptism), which belong properly to the ordained only, may be delegated, in case of necessity and then only temporarily, to the non-ordained, while other activities and roles, which also belong *properly* to the ordained only (such as presiding at Eucharist and serving as parish pastor) cannot be delegated to the non-ordained. But the non-ordained also carry out many other activities in the Church and in the world that do not *properly* belong to the ordained but that represent a participation in the mission and ministry of Christ and the Church. And many such activities we commonly refer to as ministries.

While there are ministries that are legitimately carried out in the Church by the laity, we should resist the temptation to confine lay ministries exclusively to liturgical and other "inner churchly" activities. There is a danger of clericalizing the vocation of the laity. The distinct character of the lay vocation is in the world. We may legitimately want to be more precise about the meaning of the term "ministry" and not refer to every activity of a Christian as ministry. But the terminological question is secondary. What is primary is for lay Christians to understand the call to bring the Gospel to bear in every realm of their lives.

THE CLERICAL STATE—ORDAINED TO SERVE ECCLESIAL UNITY

The state of life referred to as "clerical" encompasses those persons ordained to the diaconal, presbyteral, and episcopal ministries in the Church—deacons, priests, and bishops. Their special character is a sacramental ordination to the service of the unity of the Church. They have particular responsibilities for building up, preserving, and symbolically expressing the bonds of communion in the ecclesial body.

The participation of the ordained in the threefold ministry of Christ—prophet, priest, and king—is typically understood in ecclesial documents to take specific forms of teaching (prophet), sanctifying (priest), and governing (king) in the Church. The ordained have both sacramental and juridical authority in the Church. Their authority, however, is not to be that of dominion but rather that of service.

There are three levels or grades of ordained ministry, as we have noted: deacons, priests, and bishops. This threefold character of the Sacrament of Holy Orders has become clearer in recent years with the restoration of the permanent diaconate. But in the Church there is a similar, though not identical, threefold structure of office that is more important for understanding ecclesial organization—the roles of priest, bishop, and pope. Among these offices, that of the bishop is crucial; the other two—priest and pope—can be understood on the basis of what it means to be a bishop. Thus we now turn to a brief consideration of the office and ministry of bishops.

The Office and Ministry of Bishops

In the Catholic Church, bishops are considered to be the successors of the apostles. The episcopal office is that from which all others take their reference. The Second Vatican Council clarified that the "fullness of the sacrament of Orders" belongs to the office of bishop (*LG*, #21). Priests and deacons possess sacramental and juridical authority only to the extent that bishops share it with them. Furthermore, the pope is first of all the bishop of Rome; he does not possess a higher or fuller degree of orders than any other bishop.

The principal ministries of the bishop, according to *LG*, are teaching, sanctifying, and governing in the local church of which he is the overseer. Above all, bishops are the "visible principle and foundation of unity in their particular churches" (*LG*, #23). By definition, to be Catholic in the strict sense means that one is in communion with one's bishop. All who are in communion with the bishop are in communion with one another, and this constitutes the church of a given territory. And the communion of the universal Church is ensured by the communion of all the Catholic bishops. This communion of the bishops with one another is referred to as hierarchical communion. The bishops are members of the episcopal college and are often collectively referred to as the hierarchy. This does not mean that they are holier than other members of the Church, or that they are above other members of the Church in status or dignity. Rather, it means that they are representatives of God's holy people (from the Greek *hieros*, "holy").

Historically, the office of bishop was intimately connected to the role of presiding at the eucharistic liturgy of the local church. For example, already in the early second century, Ignatius of Antioch, a bishop and martyr, tells us that

> no one is to do anything in the church without the *episkopos*. A valid eucharist is one which is either under his presidency or the presidency of a representative appointed by him.
>
> (*Epistle to the Smyrnans*, #8)

As the churches grew and expanded, the bishop could not preside at every Eucharist, and so presbyters were authorized to preside in his stead. The primary ministry of the bishop is both sacramental and pastoral; it is to build up the communion of the Church through pastoral leadership and liturgical presidency.

The bishop has a representational role with respect to both his local diocesan church and the universal Church. The bishop represents his local church to the universal Church, and he also represents the universal Church to the local church. This dual role is ensured through his communion with all other bishops in the episcopal college. Bishops are also the authoritative teachers in matters of faith and morals within their local churches and in the universal Church. Above all, though, as the Second Vatican Council's *Decree on the Pastoral Office of Bishops in the Church (Christus Dominus, CD)* makes clear, bishops "should stand in the midst of their people as those who serve" (#16).

As with any ministry in the Church, there are charisms, gifts of the Holy Spirit, that endow persons to effectively exercise the ministry of bishop. *LG* (#4) refers to "hierarchic and charismatic gifts" bestowed on the Church by the Spirit. One might also note the list of qualifications for a bishop given in the First Letter to Timothy (3:1–7). Obviously, the talents needed for servant leadership would be particularly important for this ministry. We should note, though, that bishops (and priests) exercise authority in the Church by virtue of ordination and not simply on the basis of their personal competencies.

A primary ministry of the bishop is to orchestrate the diverse charisms and ministries of the people of his community, bringing them to the service of ever greater unity. Like the conductor of a symphony, the bishop is the focal point for the coordination of many complementary gifts. And as *LG* points out, the bishop has responsibility for the discernment of charisms in the Church:

> Judgment as to their genuinity [sic] and proper use belongs to those who are appointed leaders in the Church, to whose special competence it belongs, not indeed to extinguish the Spirit, but to test all things and hold fast to that which is good.
>
> (#12; see also 1 Thessalonians 5:12, 19–21)

Priests, in particular those who are pastors, have a role in their communities that is analogous to the role of the bishop in the diocese. The parish pastor, as the bishop's authorized representative, is the visible source and bond of unity in the parish community. Those who are in communion with him are in communion with one another, with the bishop, and with Catholics throughout the world. The ministries of the pastor are also primarily pastoral and sacramental. Historically, the ministry of this office became more cultic and focused on the liturgy than it was in the earliest period. Thus the term "presbyter," elder or leader, was replaced with "priest" (in Latin, *sacerdos*), one who offers the sacrifice, in this case, the eucharistic sacrifice. Today we are recovering a more balanced perspective by retrieving the term "presbyter," which underscores this minister's role in pastoral activity that builds up the communion of the People of God. Thus, a particularly important role also for the presbyter is to coordinate and orchestrate the charisms and ministries of the People of God in his community.

The Bishop of Rome

As the Church developed in the early period of its history, there was gradually recognized the need for some more specific means of preserving the communion of the various local churches. The bishops attempted to maintain their episcopal communion, but they came to realize that to do so they needed one among them to serve as a focal point of unity, one to whom parties in dispute or disagreement could appeal in order to resolve conflicts about Christian belief and practice. The church at Rome was recognized as having a primacy, at least among churches of the western part of the Roman Empire, due to the martyrdom in that city of the apostles Peter and Paul. Thus, the church in Rome was seen as a "first among equals," and, correspondingly, the bishop of Rome came to a position as first among equals in the college, or community, of bishops. Eventually he came to be considered as the supreme pastor of the Church, the pope.

The pope's position as first among equals in the episcopal college also goes back, of course, to the selection of Peter by Christ to be the first among equals in the body of apostles. Peter's role was to be the visible bond of unity among the apostles, to "strengthen" the brothers and sisters (Luke 22:32). Christ delegated to Peter a special role of leadership that was, again, primarily a pastoral leadership: "Feed my lambs. . . . Feed my sheep" (John 21:15–19). Technically speaking, Peter was not the first bishop of Rome; he was never referred to as *episkopos*. Still, there is a historical connection from the apostle Peter to the bishops of Rome.

The pope is considered the head of the body of bishops; still, he is not beyond the episcopal college but is one of its members. His ministry in the universal Church—the Petrine ministry—parallels that of the bishop in his local diocese. As the successor of Peter, he is "the perpetual and visible principle and foundation of unity of both the bishops and of the the faithful" (*LG*, #23). By definition, to be Catholic, one must be in communion with the bishop of Rome.

Among the ancient titles for the bishop of Rome is *pontifex maximus*, which literally means "greatest bridge-builder." The pope, the "supreme pontiff," is ultimately the visible person through whom all Christians should connect; he spans the rich diversity of the Catholic communion, reconciling it into unity. He "presides over the whole assembly of charity and protects legitimate differences, while at the same time assuring that such differences do not hinder unity, but rather contribute toward it" (*LG*, #13).

The pope exercises this ministry of unity both sacramentally and pastorally with all the bishops in communion with him. The other bishops are not his legates or vicars; they have authority in their own right. At the same time, as the history of the Church has unfolded, the exercise of this ministry has taken various forms. The primacy of the bishop of Rome is not only a primacy of honor; it is also a primacy of jurisdiction. This means that the pope is not simply a *symbol* of unity among Christians; he does act to govern the universal Church through specific directives. For example, in the current practice of the Church, the pope appoints bishops to the local churches of the world. The pope also exercises a teaching authority that is unique to his office; we shall look more closely at this in our next chapter.

In sum, to recall another ancient title, the pope is "servant of the servants of God." His ministry, like that of all the ordained, is *diakonia* for the sake of *koinonia*—service for the sake of communion.

THE CONSECRATED STATE—ESCHATOLOGICAL SIGNS OF GOD'S KINGDOM

To complete our account of states of life in the Church, we must also briefly consider those members of the Church who live as professed members of religious orders. Such persons are sometimes referred to simply as "religious"; more precisely, by the taking of a specific set of public vows they are regarded as being in the "consecrated" state.

The special character of the consecrated life is a particularly intense witness to the radical demands that the Gospel makes upon all of us. Although each religious order tends to have charisms that are particularly distinct to its way of life (e.g., Benedictines and hospitality, Dominicans and preaching), the state of religious life in general symbolizes absolute dependence on God and a certain quality of detachment from the temporal order. The life of the vowed religious is meant to point or refer to the *eschaton*, the full and complete realization of the kingdom of God (thus the term "eschatological"). By their witness, religious remind all of us in the Church that our present life and activity is ordered to a future life that God will bring about. So we must not make the affairs of this world, important as they are, absolute; only God is absolute.

Each form of life in the Church makes a unique and irreplaceable contribution to the whole of the Church's life, without which that whole would be lacking some crucial dimension. The distinctive character of every vocation—indeed, of every person in the Church—is highlighted when all are brought into coordination and communion with one another.

SUMMARY

In this chapter we have attempted to describe the structure and organization of the Church in its main features. The principal thesis is that the structure of the Church—its offices and its various forms of life—arises from and is ordered to the communion of all members with the triune God and with one another. Specific roles, offices, ministries, and ways of life in the Church arise from the gifts of the one Spirit and the mission and ministry of the one Lord.

It will be obvious that many important issues regarding Church structure and organization have not been addressed. This does not mean that these issues are not significant, only that the limitations of space have prevented their discussion. Our focus has been on the principal ways in which ecclesial life is organized.

FOR REFLECTION

1. In what ways does your faith community nurture, call forth, and develop the charisms of its members? What gifts for service has the Holy Spirit given you?

2. In your experience of the Church, do differences among members lead to greater unity, or have they more often been the occasion for division?

3. What is your understanding of servant leadership in the Church? How could this type of leadership be better exercised by you in your faith community?

CHAPTER 4

The Church— Formed Through Word and Sacrament

In previous chapters we referred to the principal means with which the Church has been endowed for the building up of ecclesial communion. These means are the proclamation of the Gospel, the celebration of the sacraments, and the exercise of pastoral leadership. These ministries correspond to the threefold office of Christ as prophet, priest, and king, in which all Christians participate. We have addressed the topic of pastoral leadership within our discussion of charisms and offices in the Church. In this present chapter we reflect on the other principal means of building ecclesial communion, that is, the proclamation of the Gospel and the celebration of the sacraments. We wish to develop the theme that the Church is "formed" through Word and sacrament.

The terms *Word* and *sacrament* are used in this chapter in the broadest senses of their meanings. In the primary sense, Jesus Christ is both Word and sacrament. Jesus is Word and sacrament of God, proclaiming and manifesting God the Father and his love among us. We shall use the terms "Word of God" and "Gospel" to refer not just to the Bible or to certain books of the New Testament but to the full and entire message of Christianity. This is the sense that we find in *Dei Verbum*, which deals with revelation and its transmission in the Church through Scripture and tradition. Here we read, for instance, that "Sacred Tradition and sacred Scripture make up a single sacred deposit of the Word of God" (#10).

In a similar manner, we shall speak of sacrament not simply in reference to the seven specific rituals in the Church that are commonly called sacraments but in the larger sense spoken of in the first paragraph of *LG*, which states that "the Church, in Christ, is in the nature of sacrament—a sign and instrument, that is, of communion with God and of unity among all. . . ."

Together, Word and sacrament make up a single "economy" of Christian revelation, that is, a single system of signs and gestures that expresses God's design for the world. Early Christian thinkers used the word "economy," which literally means "management of a household," to refer to the totality of God's plan for his created household. We should maintain a strong sense of the unity of Word and sacrament; indeed, *DV*, in speaking specifically of Scripture and the Eucharist, refers to "the table both of God's Word and of Christ's Body" (#21).

In this chapter we shall begin by examining the relationship between the Word of God and the Church. Under this heading, we shall consider how the entire Church grows and deepens in its understanding of God's Word, and how different members of the Church play diverse roles in unfolding the meaning of revelation. Then we shall turn our attention to Church and sacrament. After considering in what sense the Church may be referred to as a sacrament, we shall attend to the particular sacraments that constitute the Church's liturgical life. We shall focus especially on the Eucharist, the "sacrament of sacraments," for it is in the eucharistic assembly and Liturgy that the Church realizes its identity in the most intense way. Indeed, we shall say with the renowned twentieth-century theologian Henri de Lubac that "the Church makes the eucharist, and the eucharist makes the Church." Thus we shall see, as the *CCC* indicates, that the Church "draws her life from the word and the Body of Christ and so herself becomes Christ's Body" (#752).

The Word of God—In the Church, Above the Church

The Word of God is the entire message given in Scripture and developed and interpreted in the Christian tradition. The "Gospel" is another term that similarly refers to the full message of Christianity. While from one point of view the Word and the Gospel are proclaimed in the Church, from another and more important perspective, the Word of God is above the Church, in the sense that the Church derives its existence from the one Word who is Christ and from his proclamation of the Gospel. Although the Church, through the teaching office of the bishops (the *magisterium*), has "the task of authentically interpreting the

Word of God, whether written or handed on," still, "this teaching office [and thus the whole Church] is not above the Word of God, but serves it" (*DV*, #10).

The Church is the gathering of all those who hear the Word of God and respond to it in faith. The Gospel is the standard by which the Church's life is measured and to which the Church is accountable. And the fact is that we regularly fall short of the full vision of the Christian life presented to us in the Gospel. So, according to *LG*, the Church is "always in need of being purified" and "always follows constantly the way of penance and renewal" (*LG*, #8). Theologically, we say *ecclesia semper reformanda*, that is, the Church is always in the process of being reformed. And it is in the light of the Gospel that this continuous "re-formation" takes place. According to Yves Congar, a noted theologian of the twentieth century, the Church must regularly examine itself in the mirror of the Gospel. Indeed, movements of renewal in the history of the Church have usually involved a return to our most basic sources of faith in Scripture and tradition.

Advancing Toward the Plenitude of Divine Truth

The Church, then, has a responsibility to continually deepen its understanding of the Gospel and to live on the basis of that understanding. If, as we shall explore more fully in the next chapter, the proper vocation and essential mission of the Church is evangelization, that is, the announcement of the Gospel in the world, then clearly a prerequisite for fulfilling that mission is a continuous search for a fuller understanding of the Gospel. This search is first the responsibility of all the members of the Church, not simply those who occupy teaching offices. A crucial text that points to this responsibility is given in *DV*:

> This tradition which comes from the Apostles develop[s] in the Church with the help of the Holy

Spirit. For there is a growth in the understanding of the realities and the words which have been handed down. This happens through the contemplation and study made by believers, who treasure these things in their hearts (see Luke 2:19, 51) through a penetrating understanding of the spiritual realities which they experience, and through the preaching of those who have received through episcopal succession in the episcopate, the sure gift of truth. For as the centuries succeed one another, the Church constantly moves forward toward the fullness of divine truth, until the words of God reach their complete fulfillment in her. (#8)

This text is extremely important. The "plenitude of divine truth" is an ideal toward which the Church "makes progress" and advances. "Plenitude" simply means "fullness" or "completion." The passage indicates that at any given time in its history, the Church has a somewhat less than full and complete understanding of the Gospel, and that there is always room for further "growth in insight." As we have seen above, sometimes this growth involves correcting misunderstandings of the Gospel. Progress comes about in the first place through the pondering, study, and spiritual reflection of all members of the Church. Progress also comes about through the teaching office of the bishops, who have a special responsibility for judging whether insights truly represent advance and progress in our understanding of the Gospel message.

Dei Verbum opened up new perspectives in the Church by highlighting the historical development and evolution of our understanding of the Word of God. This document nuances two senses of fullness or plenitude as this pertains to the Gospel. On the one hand the Word of God is already fully present in our history. Christ is the "the fullness of all revelation" (#2) and he "perfected revelation by fulfilling it" (#4). Similarly, the council declares in *Unitatis Redintegratio (UR)* that the "all-embracing means of salvation" is present in the Catholic Church alone (#3).

On the other hand, our comprehension and living out of this fullness is less than complete, and so in this sense the plenitude of the Gospel lies in the future, when God will bring all of history to its culmination. As Christians, we live in the "in-between times," believing that God has fully given himself to us in Jesus and yet continuing to absorb the full impact of this gift. So our lives reflect the tension between the "already" and the "not yet" of the Gospel.

The "Sense of the Faith" (*Sensus Fidei*)

According to *LG*, the members of the Church as a whole have received a special gift of the Holy Spirit that helps them to deepen their understanding of the Gospel. This corporate gift is referred to as the *sensus fidei*, which is translated as "appreciation of the faith," meaning, according to one translator, "the instinctive sensitivity and discrimination which the members of the Church possess in matters of faith." The relevant passage is as follows:

> The entire body of the faithful, anointed as they are by the Holy One (see 1 John 2:20 and 27) cannot err in matters of belief. They manifest this special property by means of the whole peoples' supernatural discernment in matters of faith (*sensus fidei*) when, "from the Bishops down to the last of the lay faithful," they show universal agreement in matters of faith and morals. That discernment in matters of faith is aroused and sustained by the Spirit of truth. It is exercised under the guidance of the sacred teaching authority (*magisterium*), in faithful and respectful obedience to which the people of God accepts that which is not just the word of men but truly the word of God (see 1 Thessalonians 2:13). Through it, the people of God adheres unwaveringly to the faith given once and for all to the saints.
>
> (#12, see Jude 3)

This appreciation or sense of the faith is first of all a characteristic of the "whole people," who, as a whole, "cannot err in matters of belief." How are we to understand this claim, especially given the fact that, as *LG* pointed out, the Church is "always in need of being purified "(#8)? What is being referred to here is a property of the whole Church that is sometimes termed its "indefectability." This means that the Church as a whole will never "defect" (fall away) from the truth of the Gospel in a permanent and irreversible way. We have Christ's promise that we will never so lose the integral message of the Gospel that we can no longer be "re-formed" according to its truth.

As an example of the exercise of the *sensus fidei*, we might point to the declaration in 1854 by Pope Pius IX that the Immaculate Conception of Mary is a dogma, that is, a certain truth of the Catholic faith. A primary reason that this declaration could be and in fact was made is that for a very long time there had been a tradition of devotion, liturgical celebration, and theological reflection regarding Mary's immaculate conception. In other words, and this was recognized by Pius IX, the body of the faithful already had an "instinctive sensitivity" about this truth, which the pope then formally ratified in his declaration.

The *sensus fidei* obviously does not mean that any interpretation of the Gospel by an individual member or even a large group of members of the Church is necessarily correct. It is only when there is a "universal consent" of the whole people that we can be sure that we are not falling away from the Gospel. At the same time, the *sensus fidei* is not an abstraction or a purely generic quality; it does take root and develop in individual members of the Church in varying degrees. We might ask, "What are the specific ways in which this 'appreciation of the faith,' this 'instinctive sensitivity and discrimination,' develops in us?"

The *sensus fidei* is a gift of the Holy Spirit, of course, but can we say anything more about how this gift is cultivated in us? A number of theologians have observed a distinction that may be of some help. There are, according to this line of thought, two distinct ways in which we grow in knowledge and understanding of a particular subject. There is understanding that comes about through explicit study and formal observation, such as happens in a typical school classroom. But there is also understanding that comes about through participation in specific experiences and performance of particular activities.

So, for example, there is a kind of "knowing" involved in being able to swim or ride a bicycle, or many other such activities and experiences, that is not attained through formal study. The theologian Avery Dulles refers to this as knowing by "indwelling," rather than by "observation." Similarly, St. Thomas Aquinas compared knowing about moral virtue by formal study (what he called "science") and knowing about the same virtues by "connaturality," that is, by actually possessing and living out those virtues as part of one's character, one's "nature."

What we are suggesting is that the *sensus fidei* develops in us to the extent that we participate in and commit ourselves to the Christian way of life in the Church. To the degree that we give ourselves to the life of prayer, to participation in the sacramental life, to the work for justice and peace in the world, to sustained encounter and engagement with our brothers and sisters in faith, to that degree (and only to that degree) do we attain that "instinctive sensitivity" about the Gospel. We "indwell" in the Church and come to a sense of the faith that could never be arrived at simply by observing the life of the Church, as it were, from the outside. Of course, there is a valuable place for formal theological study as well; but what we have been trying to point to here is a way of seeing how the *sensus fidei* develops in all members of the Church. Through this gift, all members can contribute to the "growth in insight" and advance of the Church toward the "plenitude of divine truth."

The Whole Church, Learning and Teaching

All members of the Church are responsible for striving to understand and live out the Gospel more completely. The whole community is the Church learning, being guided by the Holy Spirit toward a more profound understanding of the Word of God. The whole community is the Church teaching, giving witness to the Word of God in many ways, including explicit catechesis and instruction.

In some theologies prior to the Second Vatican Council, the Church was divided into the teaching Church *(ecclesia docens)*, composed of the hierarchy, and the learning Church *(ecclesia discens)*, composed of everyone else. Now, while there are certainly distinctions of offices and roles in the Church, we more correctly see that we are all learners and teachers in the Church in our own proper ways.

The bishops have the responsibility of being the principal teachers of faith in their local churches and in the universal Church. Through sacramental ordination, they have become authorized teachers of the Gospel. This office that the bishops exercise—in union with the bishop of Rome, the pope, as head of the episcopal college—we refer to as the magisterium. The pope and the other bishops carry out this ministry of authoritative teaching through various specific means, such as preaching the homily, issuing pastoral letters and other documents on particular topics, and giving addresses and presentations, and in general through the witness of their entire ministry and life.

In particular, bishops are charged with the responsibility of making authoritative and binding judgments when there is disagreement or a conflict of interpretations about what the Gospel means. In the community of faith, bishops have the last word in those cases in which such a decision must be made. In this way they serve to maintain the unity of the Church. This does not mean that in every case the bishop necessarily has the deepest insight into a given matter or question but that his judgment is recognized as authoritative for the entire community. Of course, we do expect that in general the bishops are in position to have the broadest perspective and, therefore, the most well-formed judgment in matters pertaining to the life of the Church. Still, bishops must also rely on good counsel and advice, especially in questions requiring highly specialized knowledge.

The highest degree of teaching authority in the Church is exercised by the bishop of Rome as head of the body of bishops. The pope and with him the bishops offer instruction and teaching to guide and direct the whole Church. It is important to point out that there are various grades or degrees to which this teaching authority may be invoked and, correspondingly, differing types of responses that may be called for on the part of the whole body of believers. The degree to which authority is exercised depends mainly on the importance of the particular teaching in question, that is, how closely it pertains to the very foundation of Christian faith.

On certain relatively rare occasions a pope or ecumenical council of bishops may invoke their full degree of teaching authority and propose a teaching infallibly, that is, with the assurance of the Holy Spirit that a particular teaching is certainly a truth of the Gospel. In the twentieth century, there was only one occasion of an infallible teaching defined as such: the declaration of the assumption of Mary into heaven as a definite truth of the Catholic faith in 1950. In addition, according to *LG*, teachings may also be considered infallible if it can be shown that the entire communion of bishops "are in agreement on one position as definitively to be held" (#25). Most of what is essential to the Gospel, such as the resurrection of Christ, has never formally been declared infallible, mainly because it has never been deemed necessary to do so. Teachings that are proposed or considered as infallible call for the highest degree of assent from the body of the faithful; to disagree on these matters is to rupture the communion of faith.

Most of the authoritative teaching of the magisterium is of a non-infallible and nondefinitive character. The response called for in these cases is "religious submission of the mind and will" (*obsequiem religiosum*; *LG*, #25). The Latin word *obsequiem* contains a range of meanings; primarily it indicates a matter of respect, a willingness to strive to understand the teaching in question. There may be cases, however, when for well-founded reasons a member of the Church cannot assent to a nondefinitive teaching of the magisterium. A person in this situation must continue to strive to understand the truth in question and to allow his or her understanding of the issue to be corrected, if necessary, by the larger community. Respect for the teaching office of the Church must be maintained.

On the other hand, if the truth really does lie with such a person, it is his or her responsibility to loyally offer that truth to the entire community for its correction and growth. In chapter five, for example, we shall refer to the case of the American theologian John Courtney Murray, who was silenced by his superiors in the 1950s for his writings on religious freedom. Murray was vindicated at the Second Vatican Council when his views were incorporated into the council's document on religious liberty, *Dignitatis Humanae*. Murray's loyal but prophetic search for truth was crucial to the formulation of that document and helped the whole Church to "grow in insight" of the Gospel.

It is the Church as a whole that lives by the Gospel and advances toward the plenitude of divine truth. Only in the interplay of all the charisms and offices in the Church does the whole body make progress toward the truth. And it is in the truth that we all celebrate the communion to which God is calling us.

Sacraments—Signifying and Sanctifying

We now turn our attention to the theme of Church and sacrament. But in doing so we are not turning away from the Word of God; rather, we remain at the one table at which there is the most intimate relationship between Word and sacrament. In the Mass, the Liturgy of the Word and the Liturgy of the Eucharist (framed by the rites of gathering and dismissal) are not two separate liturgies but one ritual celebration. The privileged context for hearing the Word of God is the liturgical assembly.

When we think about sacrament, what is likely to come to mind first are the seven sacraments celebrated in the Church—

Baptism, Confirmation, Eucharist, Reconciliation, Anointing of the Sick, Matrimony, and Holy Orders. Each of these rites is an action performed in and by the Church. There are traditional definitions of sacrament with which we may be familiar, such as "outward signs of invisible grace," and "signs that effect what they signify."

Our word "sacrament" comes from the Latin *sacramentum*, which in turn translates the Greek work *mysterion*, meaning "mystery," that which is hidden but is beginning to be revealed. So *DV*, citing the Letter to the Ephesians (1:9–10), speaks of God making known "the hidden purpose *(sacrementum)* of His will" (*DV*, #2). This word was used in the New Testament and early Church not to designate specific rituals but to refer to God's will for his creation. And what is God's will? According to the Letter to the Ephesians, it is "to gather up all things in [Christ], things in heaven and things on earth" (1:10).

God's will, or *mysterion*, includes both the goal of communion and the means by which that communion will be achieved. Ephesians speaks of those means by referring to a "plan" (*oikonomia*, "economy," which means, as we have seen, the way in which God manages his household). What is that plan, that economy? For early Christian authors, it was clear that Christ, in whom divine and human are united, is at once the goal and the sole means of communion. So for God to make known the mystery of his will is first of all to make Christ known.

Gradually, the term *sacramentum* came to refer to specific actions in the Church by which Christ is "made known." Eventually there was a consensus to regard seven rites of the Church as sacraments. There was also some clarification about how sacraments work. Sacraments are signs by which the invisible *mysterion* is made at least partly manifest. But the sacraments are signs that actually bring about what they show. In other words, sacraments do not just inform us that God's will is for all things to be united in Christ; sacraments actually work to create or bring about that communion. That is why it is said that sacraments signify and effect, and that they effect by signifying.

The Church—Universal Sacrament of Salvation

In the process by which seven rites of the Church came to be regarded as sacraments, the original more comprehensive vision of sacrament was obscured. The documents of the Second Vatican Council, reflecting several decades of theological developments, ask us to think again in broader terms about sacrament. From this larger perspective, there is one primary sacrament in the world: Jesus Christ. For if we consider what a sacrament truly is—a visible sign through which God's gracious offer of communion is made manifest and thereby effectively present—it is clear that this is first of all true of Christ. More specifically, his humanness is the tangible, visible sign by means of which God is revealed to the world. All other meanings of sacrament derive from this one.

The human body of Christ is no longer visibly present on the earth; it is the Church, the Body of Christ, that is now visible as a sign. As Jesus is the sacrament of God the Father, so the Church is the sacrament of Christ. So *LG* tells us that "the Church is in Christ like a sacrament or as a sign and instrument both of a very closely knit union with God and of the unity of the whole human race" (#1); and again, Christ "sent His life-giving Spirit upon His disciples and through Him has established His Body which is the Church as the universal sacrament of salvation" (#48).

The salvation of which the Church is both sign and instrument is communion with God and the unity of the entire human family. The Church is an effective instrument of communion in the world precisely to the degree that it is an authentic sign of that communion in its own life. That is why the internal divisions of Christianity are so damaging to the mission of the Church in the world. How can we invite the world into our communion when we ourselves are not one? Here we are speaking especially of the lack of full communion among Catholic, Orthodox, and Protestant Christians but also of the discord and lack of charity that sometimes exists among members of the

Catholic Church. Again, unity does not mean uniformity but rather the harmony of reconciled diversity.

We see once more the close interplay between communion and mission in understanding the Church. Being sacramental people means that in our lives we will work to bring about greater unity and communion, a greater mutual sharing of gifts, in the Church and the world. The celebration of the sacraments should spill over into every part of our lives, permeating our experiences in family, at work, in the neighborhood, and in the wider world. In this way, we ourselves will be signs and instruments of God's plan of communion for the world.

So the Church is called to be the universal sacrament of salvation, that is, the sign, means, and fruit of communion among all the peoples and cultures of the world with God and one another. Only in this way is the Church truly catholic, which means "according to the whole," or "universal." We shall have more to say about the catholicity of the Church in chapter seven.

Sacraments—By the Church, For the Church

The Church—more precisely, the local assembly of believers—both expresses ("signifies") and thereby realizes ("effects") itself in its sacramental and liturgical life. Here is how the *CCC* describes this twofold process:

> The sacraments are "of the Church" in the double sense that they are "by her" and "for her." They are "by the Church," for she is the sacrament of Christ's action at work in her through the mission of the Holy Spirit. They are "for the Church" in the sense that "the sacraments make the Church,"[1] since they manifest and communicate to men, above all in the Eucharist, the mystery of communion with the God who is love, One in three persons. (#1118)

We emphasize that it is the whole community of Christians that is the primary celebrant of all liturgical actions; within this unity, specific members have particular roles, but what comes first is the action of the entire assembly. Again the *CCC* states, "It is the whole *community*, the Body of Christ united with its Head, that celebrates" (#1140). The Second Vatican Council's *Constitution on the Sacred Liturgy (Sacrosanctum Concilium, SC)* reminds us

> that liturgical services are not private functions but are celebrations of the Church, which is the "sacrament of unity," namely, "the holy people united and arranged under their bishops."
>
> Therefore, liturgical services pertain to the whole Body of the Church. They manifest it, and have effects upon it. But they also touch individual members of the Church in different ways, depending on their orders, their role in the liturgical services, and their actual participation in them. (#26)

Eucharistic Ecclesiology

All of the sacraments, each in its own way, help to make the Church. Baptism is a fundamental means of helping to make the Church; through this rite persons explicitly join the community of faith. So we say that Baptism incorporates persons into the body of Christ. Confirmation further manifests the gifts of the Spirit in the members of the Church. Reconciliation and Anointing work to heal the body and to strengthen it in the face of sin and human frailty. Matrimony and Holy Orders are "sacraments at the service of communion and the mission of the faithful" (*CCC*, #1211).

At the same time, it is the Eucharist that in a pre-eminent way makes the Church. This sacrament, which indeed we call "Communion," at once symbolizes and creates the communion of God the Father, through Christ, in the Spirit, with us. This theme, which was very prominent among the Church fathers, has been rediscovered in our time. Here is how St. Augustine preached on the topic to his community:

> "The Body of Christ," you are told, and you answer "Amen." Be members then of the Body of Christ that your amen may be true. Why is this mystery accomplished with bread? We shall say nothing of our own about it, rather let us hear the Apostle [Paul], who, speaking of this sacrament says: "We, being many, are one body, one bread" [1 Corinthians 10:17]. . . . At baptism you were wetted with water. Then the Holy Spirit came into you like the fire which bakes the dough. Be then what you see and receive what you are.
>
> (St. Augustine, *Sermons*, #272, 234)

Unlike other food that we eat, which becomes part of our physical body, in the Eucharist we are transformed into that which we eat. For Augustine, it is as if Christ says to us: "You will not change me into you, but you will be changed into me" (St. Augustine, *Confessions*). Remembering that the ultimate purpose of the Eucharist is to transform those who are assembled at the table gives us the proper context for understanding the transformation of the bread and wine into the Body and Blood of Christ.

At a number of points the documents of the Second Vatican Council remind us that the Eucharist helps make the Church. For example, *LG* tells us that "in the sacrament of the eucharistic bread, the unity of all believers who form one body in Christ (see 1 Corinthians 10:17) is both expressed and brought about" (#3). And *SC* recalls for us the vision of the early second century bishop and martyr, Ignatius of Antioch:

> All should hold in the greatest esteem the liturgical life of the diocese centered around the bishop, especially in his cathedral church; they must be convinced that the pre-eminent manifestation of

the Church consists in the full active participation of all God's holy people in these liturgical celebrations, especially in the same eucharist, in a single prayer, at one altar, at which there presides the bishop, surrounded by his college of priests and by his ministers. (#41)

If Christ is the sacrament of God, and the Church is the sacrament of Christ, then the Eucharist is the sacrament of the Church. But for this to truly be so, for the Church to truly be the Body of Christ, the eucharistic table must be a place of full inclusion. All of us properly, and not just by convention, say "Lord, I am not worthy to receive you. But only say the word, and I shall be healed." The Eucharist does not abolish differences between people, but it should transcend and reconcile them. The eucharistic table is a place of communion for all people: persons of different classes, races, genders, occupations, ideologies, sexual orientations, ages, and abilities.

As the Eucharist is the sacrament of the Church, so our lives in the world are meant to be the sacrament of the Eucharist, in that our lives manifest and bring about the communion we celebrate in the eucharistic Liturgy. The nature of the Eucharist is violated if we fail to recognize its consequences for our lives in the world. We cannot share the eucharistic bread without sharing our daily bread as well. To "be what we see and receive," that is, to be "Eucharist," we must practice eucharistic hospitality in the world, welcoming strangers and embracing the outcasts, just as Jesus did.

So the eucharistic Liturgy, as we noted in the introduction, does not close in on itself; rather, just the opposite is the case. The eucharistic assembly ends with the sending out into the world for mission of those who had gathered. As the German bishop Walter Kasper puts it:

Gathering and sending forth are two poles that must not be separated or played off against one another. Without the gathering, the going forth becomes inwardly empty and hollow; but the gathering without the going forth becomes sterile and ultimately unconvincing.

(Theology and Church, p. 191)

Finally, we should recognize that the celebration of the Eucharist on earth is also a sign and foretaste of the banquet awaiting us in the life to come. The Church will only fully become what it is meant to be in the future fulfillment of all things by God that we refer to as heaven. So even now our eucharistic Liturgies anticipate the heavenly banquet, which Jesus likened to a marriage feast, in which full communion will be experienced. As the Orthodox theologian John Zizoulas puts it, the Church "is what she is by becoming again and again what she will be." This future banquet, and this future Church, though, is not purely future; it is already beginning to be realized as often as we eat the bread and drink the cup of the Lord until he comes again (see 1 Corinthians 11:26).

Summary

In this chapter we have explored the "coming-to-be" of the Church through Word and sacrament. The intimate connection of these gifts for unity is emphasized in a particularly apt way in the Second Vatican Council's *Decree on the Ministry and Life of Priests (Presbyterorum Ordinis, PO)*. On the one hand, "the People of God is formed into one in the first place by the Word of the living God. . . . The preaching of the Word is required for the sacramental ministry itself, since the sacraments are sacraments of faith, drawing their origin and nourishment from the Word" (#4). On the other hand, "all ecclesiastical ministries and works of the apostolate are bound up with the Eucharist and are directed towards it. . . . The Eucharist appears as the source and the summit of all preaching of the Gospel" (#5).

We see how the ministries of Word and sacrament correspond to the prophetic and priestly offices of Christ and also to the teaching and sanctifying ministries in the Church. But we have also seen that Word and sacrament lead the believing and worshiping assembly beyond the sanctuary and out into the world, so that all may be brought into full communion with God. In the following chapters we shall turn to the mission of the Church in the world, beginning in chapter five with a study of evangelization.

ENDNOTE

1. St. Augustine, *De civ. Dei*, 22, 17: PL 41, 779; cf. St. Thomas Aquinas, *STh* III, 64, 2 *ad* 3.

FOR REFLECTION

1. How do you see yourself contributing to the advance and progress of the Church toward the "plenitude of divine truth"?

2. What is your understanding of the relationship between Word and sacrament?

3. How does your faith community help its members to be sacraments of eucharistic communion and hospitality in the world?

CHAPTER 5

The Mission of the Church— Evangelizing Cultures

I n the first part of this book, we focused our attention on the inner life of the Church. Our primary aim was to describe ecclesial communion, to indicate the visible structure of that communion in its diversity and complementarity, and to explain how that communion is built up through the ministries of Word and sacrament. But as we have seen, gathering always leads to sending; indeed, without the sending forth for mission in the world, our gathering and communion in the eucharistic assembly are compromised and lacking. In this chapter, then, we begin to reflect in explicit detail on the essential missionary nature of the Church.

To be sure, though, the purpose of mission is to increase and enrich communion, to make it more inclusive. The goal of mission is the gathering of all people around the Lord's table. From this point of view, the first missionary act of the Church is simply to be an authentic witness of communion in its inner life. As Pope John Paul II notes in his important letter on the Church's missionary mandate, *On the Permanent Validity of the Church's Missionary Mandate (Redemptoris Missio, RM),*

> The ultimate purpose of mission is to enable people to share in the communion which exists between the Father and the Son. . . . We are missionaries above all because of what we are as a Church, whose innermost life is unity in love, even before we become missionaries in word or deed. (#23)

It is the entire Church, with each and every individual member, that is missionary by its very nature. Of course, there are some members of the Church who have a more immediately recognizable call to mission in the traditional sense of proclaiming the Gospel among non-Christian peoples. But we are being challenged now to think of mission in the broad sense, in which we all participate in one form or another. The *CCC* makes this clear:

> The whole Church is apostolic, in that she remains, through the successors of St. Peter and the other

apostles, in communion of faith and life with her origin: and in that she is "sent out" into the whole world. All members of the Church share in this mission, though in various ways. "The Christian vocation is, of its nature, a vocation to the apostolate as well."[1]

We might say, then, that in a certain sense the Church is not only a communion of disciples but is also a communion of apostles, in that as Christians each of us is sent forth into the world in a specific form of mission. The Second Vatican Council's *Decree on the Apostolate of Lay People (Apostolicam Actuositatem, AA)*, actually says, "The laity derive the right and duty to the apostolate from their union with Christ the head." (#3)

Granted that the overall goal of mission is the increase of communion, and that this applies to everything that Christians do in the world, still, we wish to be more specific about what exactly the mission of the Church is. To begin, then, we note that the one mission of the Church has two distinct but inseparable components: first, the announcement of the Gospel; and second, in light of and as a consequence of that announcement, the development and improvement of human society on earth, what is called in conciliar documents "the Christian formation of the temporal order."

In the present chapter, we examine the primary mission of the Church—the announcement of the Gospel, or evangelization. In recent years, we have been challenged to view all Christian ministries and activities as forms of evangelization. In the chapter to follow, we shall take up the secondary component of the Church's mission, namely, the contribution of the Church toward personal and social development in the world. It must be stressed, though, that these two components cannot be separated; evangelization and human development form one integral mission of the Church.

Evangelization—Deepest Identity of the Church

One of the most striking developments in Catholic thought since the Second Vatican Council is the prominence given to the theme of evangelization. A generation ago, Catholics might well have shied away from using this term, associating it with pushy proselytizing and the highly charged preaching of charismatic ministers. But we have since come to reclaim the deepest and original sense of the word "evangelization," which comes from the Greek word for Gospel *(euangelion)*, meaning "good message" or "good news." Evangelization, then, is any means by which the Gospel is communicated and put into practice—not just enthusiastic preaching but every form of witness and ministry in the Christian life, including catechesis, pastoral care, and liturgy. Indeed, we must speak of evangelization as a complex and dynamic process in which there are many elements or moments, a process, in fact, that is never entirely completed.

We have come to a clearer understanding that evangelization is the essential mission of the Church, indeed, the very reason for the Church to exist. In 1975, Pope Paul VI published an apostolic exhortation entitled *On Evangelization in the Modern World (Evangelii Nuntiandi, EN)*, a landmark document that presented a vision of the Church as the evangelizing community. Here is how he speaks of evangelization and the Church:

> "We wish to confirm once more that the task of evangelizing all people constitutes the essential mission of the Church." It is a task and mission which the vast and profound changes of present-day society make all the more urgent. Evangelizing is in fact the grace and vocation proper to the Church, her deepest identity. She exists in order to evangelize.
>
> (#14, citing the 1974 Synod of Bishops)

As we indicated in the previous chapter, the Church can only evangelize effectively to the extent that it continually seeks to deepen and advance its own understanding and living out of the Gospel. Another way of saying this is that the first task for the Church is to be evangelized itself. The community of believers, corporately and individually, "has a constant need of being evangelized, if she wishes to retain freshness, vigor and strength in order to proclaim the Gospel" (*EN*, #15). The Church "is evangelized by constant conversion and renewal, in order to evangelize the world with credibility" (*EN*, #15).

In 1992 the National Conference of Catholic Bishops in the United States issued *Go and Make Disciples (GMD)*, a "plan and strategy of evangelization" for the Church of the United States. Following up on *EN*, *GMD* calls on every member of the Church to take up, each in his or her own way, the task of evangelization, which is essential to being a Christian. The plan offers three main goals and suggests strategies for working toward each goal:

> Goal I: To bring about in all Catholics such an enthusiasm for their faith that, in living their faith in Jesus, they freely share it with others.

> Goal II: To invite all people in the United States, whatever their social or cultural background, to hear the message of salvation in Jesus Christ so they may come to join us in the fullness of the Catholic faith.

> Goal III: To foster gospel values in our society, promoting the dignity of the human person, the importance of the family, and the common good of our society, so that our nation may continue to be transformed by the saving power of Jesus Christ.

Clearly, goals II and III correspond to the two distinct but inseparable components of mission spoken of above—announcing the Gospel and transforming society. Goal I is the indispensable prerequisite for this mission—that we ourselves as Church are continually renewed, reformed, and evangelized.

The Essential Moments of Evangelization

The entire mission of the Church and its many ministries should be viewed as essential elements in the complex and rich process of evangelization. The *General Directory for Catechesis (GDC)* certainly places Christian formation within the broader scope of evangelization. The first part of that document is entitled "Catechesis in the Church's Mission of Evangelization." The "catechetical moment" is one of several distinct but intimately connected moments that taken as a whole make up evangelization.

The whole of evangelization is aimed at conversion, the ongoing transformation of persons, societies, and cultures in the light of the Gospel. The *GDC*, in paragraph 48, tells us that evangelization "is urged by *charity*," that it "bears *witness*" and proclaims the Gospel, that it "*initiates*" followers of Jesus into Christian faith and life, and that it is concerned with nourishing the mission and communion of the Church.

The several distinct moments that are essential to the process of evangelization are perhaps most clearly illustrated in the Rite of Christian Initiation of Adults (RCIA). The full scope of the RCIA basically corresponds to the full range of evangelization (see *GDC*, #88). Each of the distinct moments is intrinsically ecclesial, that is, an act of the Church, even when carried out by individual members (see *EN*, #20–24; *GDC*, #36–76).

First, there is the initial act of evangelization, which is simply the witness of a genuine Christian life, a life inspired by the Gospel. "Above all the Gospel must be proclaimed by witness" (#21). It is when people can say of Christians, "See how they love one another," that there is created a moment of interest in the Gospel.

Second, there is the explicit proclamation of the Gospel, the initial presentation of the message of Christianity in explicit form. Such proclamation leads ideally to a first step of conversion on the part of its recipients, a first assimilation to the message of Jesus. The changes taking place in persons should have their social effects as well, so that not only the individual but society as well begins to undergo transformation according to the values of the Gospel. These first two moments correspond to the period of evangelization and precatechumenate of the RCIA, also known as the period of inquiry.

Third, there is an initial period of formation, an "apprenticeship in the whole Christian life," which includes instruction that is "comprehensive, organic, and systematic." This is referred to as "initiatory catechesis" and corresponds to the catechumenate of the RCIA. This catechesis "promotes and matures initial conversion, educates the convert in the faith and incorporates him into the Christian community" (*GDC*, #61). Baptismal catechesis is "the model for all catechesis," and "should inspire the other forms of catechesis in both their objectives and in their dynamism" (*GDC*, #59; see also 1977 Synod of Bishops, *Message to the People of God*, #8).

Fourth, there is the moment of sacramental initiation into the community of faith, through Baptism, Confirmation, and Eucharist, which occurs most properly at the Easter Vigil. "Thus those whose life has been transformed enter a community which is itself a sign of transformation, a sign of newness of life: it is the Church, the visible sacrament of salvation." (*EN*, #23)

Fifth, there is continuing formation in the ecclesial community. This is referred to as "catechesis at the service of ongoing formation in the faith" (*GDC*, #69). Regularly nourished at the one table of Gospel and Eucharist, Christians mature in their faith through continual conversion, assisted by multiple forms of ongoing catechesis, such as Scripture study, liturgical catechesis, and theological instruction. "The action of the Holy Spirit operates so that the gift of 'communion' and the task of 'mission' are deepened and lived in an increasingly intense way" (*GDC*, #70). This moment would correspond to the period of mystagogy, or post-baptismal catechesis, in the RCIA.

Finally, the evangelized becomes the evangelizer:

> Here lies the test of truth, the touchstone of evangelization: it is unthinkable that a person should accept the Word and give himself to the kingdom without becoming a person who bears witness to it and proclaims it in his turn. (*EN*, #24)

So the process comes full circle, as persons evangelized into the communion of faith take up specific forms of mission in order to bring others to that same communion.

Evangelization is thus "a complex process made up of varied elements" that "may appear to be contradictory, indeed mutually exclusive. In fact they are complementary and mutually enriching. Each one must always be seen in relationship with the others" (*EN*, #24). This whole process is how disciples are made. And that is the missionary mandate of Christ: Go and make disciples.

The New Evangelization

The Church has been evangelizing from its very beginnings. Obviously, the Church would have never grown beyond its initial numbers had the first disciples not witnessed to and proclaimed the Gospel. Otherwise, we ourselves would have never heard the message. At the same time, there is something new about the recent emphasis on evangelization. Building upon the vision of Pope Paul VI, Pope John Paul II has called the Church to a "new evangelization"—"new in ardor, methods, and expression." The concept of the "new evangelization" includes everything that we have been speaking of so far in this chapter. Here we wish to summarize its main themes.

The traditional understanding of missionary activity is that it is directed *ad gentes*, that is, "to the peoples," to those regions and parts of societies where Christ and the Gospel are not yet known or where the Church has not yet taken root. The mission *ad gentes* is "the exemplary model" for all the Church's missionary activity (*GDC*, #59), but it does not exhaust what we need to do. There is also, as we have seen, the need for continuing evangelization of already existing Christian communities, so that the Gospel may have an even deeper influence in the lives of practicing Christians. Third, there is a need for re-evangelization of persons and entire groups of peoples and regions who have received the Gospel but who have lost a living sense of the faith and no longer consider

themselves members of the Church. The need to address the phe-
nomenon of "de-Christianization" is a particularly new feature of
the "new evangelization" (see *RM*, #33; *GDC*, #58).

What else is "new" about evangelization? Theologian Avery
Dulles lists seven essential features of evangelization as it has
come to be understood in the contemporary Church:

1. Distinction of three "situations" for evangelization, as
described above

2. Active participation of all members of the Church, and not
just a few specialized persons, in evangelization

3. Acceptance of religious freedom. Persons freely decide to
accept the Gospel and join the Church; evangelization is a matter of invitation, not coercion

4. Recognition that new hearers of the Gospel already have a
certain degree of religious experience in their lives; there are
"seeds of the Gospel" already present. When we evangelize, we
listen and learn, as well as proclaim and teach

5. Evangelization of cultures as well as persons (we shall give
more attention to this theme below)

6. Evangelization includes efforts to make society more just (we
shall take up this topic in more detail in our next chapter)

7. Utilization of new forms of media made available by technology. This is not simply a matter of using the media to communi-
cate the Christian message but of integrating that message into
the "new culture" created by modern communications. (Dulles,
"Seven Essentials of Evangelization," *Origins* 25:23 [23
November 1995])

The Evangelization of Cultures

A principal feature of the new evangelization is the recognition
that cultures and not just individuals must be brought under the

influence of the Gospel. Paul VI clearly articulated this point when he stated that

> the split between the Gospel and culture is without a doubt the drama of our time, just as it was of other times. Therefore every effort must be made to ensure a full evangelization of culture, or more correctly, of cultures. They have to be regenerated by an encounter with the Gospel. But this encounter will not take place if the Gospel is not proclaimed.
>
> (*EN*, #20)

Here Pope Paul is building on the perspectives of the Second Vatican Council's *Pastoral Constitution on the Church in the Modern World (Gaudium et Spes, GS)*. This document suggests a reciprocal relationship between persons and cultures: persons create cultures, but cultures form persons. Thus "men and women. . . are the authors and artisans of the culture of their community" (*GS*, #55), while at the same time the human person can realize "true and full humanity only through culture" (*GS*, #53). This indicates that persons acquire their values largely by absorbing them from the various cultures in which they live. So if evangelization involves transforming the values by which we live, it must at the same time address the cultures that so powerfully and pervasively form us.

Pope John Paul II embraced the idea of the evangelization of cultures and made it one of the major themes of his pontificate. In 1982 he created the Pontifical Council for Culture, an advisory body intended to give "to the whole Church a common impulse in the incessant encounter of the Gospel's message of salvation with the plurality of cultures." In fact, the Gospel, and likewise the Church, can only take root and grow within particular cultural settings, even though it cannot be identified with any one culture. A faith that does not fully penetrate the fabric of a given culture is one that has not been fully received and lived out.

What Are Cultures?

Before speaking any further of cultures, we should ask, "What exactly is a culture?" This is a term that we use in many senses. First, perhaps, we think of broad national and ethnic cultures— French or Arabic, for example, or Hispanic and African American. Second, within these larger entities there are various distinct sublevels and groupings so that within American culture (meaning here the culture of the United States) we refer to the Midwest, or the South, or Appalachia not simply in geographical terms but as regions whose people have some distinct identifying traits. Third, there are cultures associated with different occupations and classes of people so that we hear terms such as "corporate culture" or "middle-class culture." Fourth, there is the aesthetic notion of culture, referring more specifically to the world of the arts and entertainment. So we might distinguish "pop" culture from "highbrow" culture. Finally, the term can refer to almost any recognizable set of beliefs, values, symbols, and practices, regardless of how such a distinct pattern arises. So, for example, authors refer to the "culture of narcissism" or the "television culture." Pope John Paul II contrasts the "culture of life" and the "culture of death" (see the encyclical *Evangelium Vitae*). And there are many other phrases in which the term is used ("clerical culture," "youth culture," etc.).

Can we bring any more definition to the concept of culture? Basically, there are two approaches that can be taken. On the one hand, there is the sense of culture emphasizing the ideals to which we should aspire. Thus we speak of "cultured" persons, those who represent the highest achievements of a given society; this is to be cultured in the classical sense as opposed to being barbarous or vulgar. This we call the *normative* or *prescriptive* view of culture. On the other hand, there is the sense of culture that simply describes how a given group of people do in fact live, regardless of how they could live. From this point of view a "culture" is any set of attitudes and values that can be acquired, transmitted, and expressed in behavior, rituals, symbols, beliefs, etc., and that constitute part of the identity of a particular group of people. This we call the *empirical* or *descriptive* view of culture.

Now what sense of culture do we mean when we speak about the evangelization of cultures? *Gaudium et Spes* seems to draw on both main senses of the term in its discussion of culture:

> The word "culture" in the general sense refers to all those things which go to the refining and developing of man's diverse mental and physical endowments. . . . Hence it follows that culture necessarily has historical and social overtones, and the word "culture" often carries with it sociological and ethnological connotations; in this sense one can speak about a plurality of cultures. For different styles of living and different scales of values originate in different ways of using things, of working and self-expression, of practicing religion and of behavior, of establishing laws and juridical institutions, of developing science and the arts and of cultivating beauty. (#53)

The Gospel is meant to address all types of cultures and to come to expression in many distinct cultural forms. So we respect and work with the descriptive notion of culture. At the same time, the Gospel is meant not simply to be expressed in different cultural forms but to "trans-form" all cultures, that is, to build up and develop everything that is good about a culture while purifying it of those elements not in line with Gospel values. Through their cultures, men and women are refined and developed. So there is a place as well for the more prescriptive sense of culture.

We have engaged in this discussion about what a culture is because of the importance given today to the evangelization of cultures. Indeed, Pope John Paul II further expanded our understanding by speaking also of the need to evangelize distinct "cultural sectors." By this he meant those distinct spheres and institutions in society that are so crucial in human formation, such as higher education, the communications media, and science and technology. All cultures are arenas that should be infused with the values of the Gospel.

Transforming the Cultures
of the United States

Because this book is intended for an audience within the United States of America, we shall speak of the cultural properties of the United States that are to be transformed by the power of the Gospel. That transformation involves a twofold movement, as the *GDC* states: "In the light of the Gospel, the Church must appropriate all the positive values of culture and of cultures and reject those elements which impede development of the true potential of persons and peoples" (*GDC*, #21; see *EN*, #20; and *On Catechesis in Our Time [Catechesi Tradendae]*, #53).

We live in a very complex and pluralistic society, and so our considerations must necessarily be quite general. Many cultural groupings and subgroupings exist within the larger culture of the United States. Every person belongs to any number of such cultures, some broader and more comprehensive, others more narrow and limited. The different cultures that we belong to are based, as we have seen, on where we live, our ethnic background, our occupations and interests, etc. The national plan of evangelization, *GMD*, offers some general observations about what is good and bad in the broad culture of the United States:

> Not only must each of us live the Gospel personally in the Church, but our faith must touch the values of the United States, affirming what is good, courageously challenging what is not. Catholics applaud our nation's instinctual religiousness, its prizing of freedom and religious liberty, its openness to new immigrants, and its inspiring idealism. If our society were less open, indeed, we might not be free to evangelize in the first place. On the other hand, our country can be faulted for its materialism, sexism, racism, consumerism, its individualism run wild, its ethic of selfishness, its ignoring of the poor and weak, its disregard of human life, and its endless chase of empty fads and immediate pleasures.

Seeing both the ideals and the faults of our nation, we Catholics need to recognize how much our Catholic faith, for all it has received from American culture, still has to bring to life in our country. On the level of truth, we have a profound and consistent moral teaching based upon the dignity and destiny of every person created by God. On the practical level we have the witness of American Catholics serving those most in need, educationally, socially, materially, and spiritually. (p. 9)

In his pastoral visits to the United States, Pope John Paul II has also brought a sharp and discriminating perspective on what is good and bad in American culture. He has addressed the dominant culture of our country, particular minority subcultures such as the Hispanic, Native American, and African-American communities, and cultural sectors such as the business community and the media. He applauds, among other things, the cultural values of freedom, multicultural pluralism, and the generosity of the American people. At the same time he challenges this country to create a "culture of life" that respects the dignity of all persons, to maintain the right of minority cultures to a distinct cultural development and the preservation of their heritage, and to avoid the secularism and consumerism that threaten us as byproducts of our prosperity. It is up to every local church in the United States, each in its particular cultural milieu but in communion with one another and the universal Church, to take up its mission of the evangelization of cultures.

The Inculturation of the Gospel and the Church

We may have given the impression that the interaction of the Gospel and the Church with cultures is primarily a one-way street, with the Gospel affecting cultures but itself remaining largely unchanged in the process. The evangelization of cultures, however, always involves at the same time the *inculturation* of the Gospel and the Church. We now turn our attention to some important principles of inculturation.

Our first source again is *GS*. To begin with, two equally important principles must be held together. First, there is no one culture that is normative or innately superior to others in offering possibilities for the embodiment of the Word of God. All cultures offer distinct but limited possibilities for the concrete expression of the Gospel and for the advance and progress of our understanding of the Gospel toward the plenitude of truth. Because each culture's contribution can only be partial, it is imperative, in order for the Church to become fully catholic, that all cultures be evangelized so that each may make its specific contributions. According to *GS*:

> The Church, sent to all peoples of every time and place, is not bound exclusively and indissolubly to any race or nation, any particular way of life or any customary way of life recent or ancient. Faithful to her own tradition and at the same time conscious of her universal mission, she can enter into communion with the various civilizations, to their enrichment and the enrichment of the Church herself. (#58)

The second principle is that the Gospel and the Church can exist only as embodied within particular cultures. Just as the Son of God, in order to share our humanness, had to take flesh in a particular human body at a given place and time (and culture) within human history, so the Word of God is present only in specific embodiments, though it is not identical to any one of them. Again, *GS* states:

> There are many ties between the message of salvation and human culture. For God, revealing Himself to His people to the extent of a full manifestation of Himself in His Incarnate Son, has spoken according to the culture proper to each epoch. Likewise the Church, living in various circumstances

in the course of time, has used the discoveries of different cultures so that in her preaching she might spread and explain the message of Christ to all nations, that she might examine and more deeply understand it, and that she might give it better expression in liturgical celebration and in the varied life of the community of the faithful. (#58)

The different contributions of the various cultures of the world to the expression and realization of the Gospel represent another type of mutual sharing of gifts that is the hallmark of communion. Like different persons, different cultures need the gifts of others to make up for what they lack and to correct deficiencies and shortcomings. To give an example, the teaching of the Second Vatican Council that every person has an inviolable right to choose a religious faith based on his or her conscience represents a special contribution of the American church to the universal Church. It was an American theologian, John Courtney Murray, reflecting upon the unique history and experience of the United States, with its constitutional guarantee of religious liberty (the "free exercise" clause of the First Amendment) and the absence of an official state religion (the "non-establishment" clause), who was instrumental in advancing Catholic doctrine on religious freedom (see the council's *Declaration on Religious Liberty*). This contribution was made possible by the particular experiences of our culture, which include religious pluralism and toleration and the absence of a long history of entanglement between church and state.

The local churches of the various cultures of the world are called to be the primary agents of evangelization and inculturation. Through them, cultures are enriched and renewed by the Gospel, and the Church is enriched in its communion and diversity. "Through inculturation the Church, for her part, becomes a more intelligible sign of what she is and a more effective instrument of mission" (*RM*, #52).

Summary

In this chapter we have explored the primary mission of the Church. We have seen how the Catholic Church has embraced the concept of evangelization and developed a vision of its life based on this theme. We have also noted the important relationship between evangelization and cultures, and have indicated the need for inculturation in order to allow the richness of the Gospel message to be manifest in its fullness. In our next chapter, we will look at a second essential dimension of the mission of the Church, namely, its contribution to human progress and social development in the world.

Endnote

1. *CCC* 863: *AA 2 (Apostolicam Actuositatem, Decree on the Apostolate of Lay People)*

For Reflection

1. In what ways does being a Christian involve being apostolic and evangelizing for you? Do you believe that your faith community is sufficiently missionary?

2. What are the cultures that form you and your life? What are the cultures within which you minister?

3. What are the positive characteristics of these cultures, and in what areas do they need to be challenged by the Gospel?

CHAPTER 6

The Mission of the Church— Transforming the World

The single mission of the Church is to evangelize, to proclaim the Gospel in the world. But this one mission has two distinct though inseparable tasks. The first and foremost task is to announce God's offer of salvation in Word and sacrament and to invite people into a relationship with Christ, in the Spirit, as sons and daughters of God the Father and brothers and sisters to one another. Second, and as a consequence of this announcement, the Church has the mission of infusing into secular society (the "world" or the "temporal order") the values of the Gospel. In a frequently used image, the Gospel is to be the leaven of human society and the world, permeating every facet and aspect of life on earth with the flavor and values of the kingdom of God.

Lay persons in the Church are called in a particular way to infuse Gospel values into society. Because of their positions and occupations in the world, they have the opportunity, in varying degrees, of shaping family life, civic life, the economy, and other dimensions of human society according to the light of the Gospel. In fact, the Second Vatican Council's document on the laity is one of the texts of the council that describes the twin tasks of evangelization:

> The work of Christ's redemption concerns essentially the salvation of [humankind]; it takes in also, however, the renewal of the whole temporal order. The mission of the Church, consequently, is not only to bring [humankind] the message and grace of Christ but also to permeate and improve the whole range of the temporal. (*AA*, #5)

The goal of this chapter is to explain the relationship between the Church and the world. We shall reflect on the pilgrim status of the Church in the world, keeping in mind that our final goal is a "new heaven and a new earth" that is more than just the achieving of a perfect or utopian world in our present life. Finally, we shall look at the principal themes of Catholic social teaching, that rich body of thought that has been referred to as "our best kept secret."

The Church—In the World But Not of the World

Christians are called to be "in the world but not of the world." So the same can be said of the Church. In a sense, this is the greatest challenge of the Christian life: to continually discern and to embody in practice this perspective of being in the world but not of the world. We must seek to maintain a dynamic balance between the "in" and the "not of."

On either side of this dynamic balance, there are extremes that distort the message of the Gospel. On the one hand, one could understand Christianity in such an other-worldly way that we lose any real sense of being "in" this world. Being a Christian then looks more like an escape from the world rather than an engagement with it. The Church then appears as nothing but a refuge from this "vale of tears." What results is a situation in which faith has no impact on daily life and the society in which we live is untouched by the influence of the Gospel. We refer to this situation as one of *dualism*; that is, there is a sharp dichotomy and separation between the sacred and the secular, between faith and daily life, between Church and world, and between the message of the Gospel and the aspirations, desires, and affairs of people in this world.

On the other hand, one could so identify Christianity with improving the quality of life on earth that any real sense of life beyond this world is lost. From this point of view, there is little to distinguish the Church from other social and political organizations that are trying to improve our lot in the world. Being a Christian then simply means having a humanitarian spirit, and salvation is conceived without any reference to the life of the world to come. This perspective loses sight of the "not of" part of being a genuine Christian. This interpretation of Christianity could be termed *reductionism*, in that the meaning of the Gospel is reduced to a purely this-worldly message.

Both dualism and reductionism are extremes to be avoided. In the history of Christianity, though, the more frequent problem seems to be dualism, the separation of faith from daily life and the world. In some ways such a separation characterized much of Catholic life in the years prior to the Second Vatican Council. Now, on the one hand, Catholics were quite engaged in the world during this period; various movements and associations, such as the Christian Family Movement and the Catholic Worker, were already bringing the Gospel to bear on family and social life well before the council.

On the other hand, though, many expressions of Catholic spirituality and life before the Second Vatican Council were decidedly dualistic. For example, marriage and family life, to say nothing of the single vocation, was regularly portrayed as a less exalted vocation than priesthood and religious life. The ordained and consecrated states were the real paths to holiness, while those with a vocation "in the world" could never be as holy. In the *Baltimore Catechism* (1962), there is a drawing of a couple before the altar at their wedding Mass with the heading, "This is Good," and the caption, "I want to marry the person of my choice." This drawing is set next to a drawing of a religious sister praying before an altar, with the heading, "This is Better," and the caption "I choose Christ as my spouse." An explanation is given about the "superiority of virginity and celibacy over the married state."

One could expect to believe that the superiority of celibacy to marriage is no longer the teaching of the Church. *Lumen Gentium* spoke of the universal call to holiness and, as we noted earlier, Pope John Paul II, in his letter on the laity, taught that what distinguished persons in the Church is "not an increase in dignity but a special and complementary capacity for service" (*CL*, #20). Thus, it comes as something of a surprise to discover that some recent documents continue to claim that celibacy and virginity are innately superior to marriage. In a letter entitled *On the Role of the Christian Family in the Modern World (Familiaris Consortio, FC)*, Pope John Paul II states that "the Church throughout her history has always defended the superiority of this charism (celibacy) to that of marriage, by reason of the wholly singular link which it has with the kingdom of God" (#16).

One must ask whether there is some contradiction and some remnant of dualism implied in this statement.

The Church "in" the Modern World— *Gaudium et Spes* and Beyond

It is indeed a challenge and an adventure to live as a Christian "in the world but not of the world." The easier path would be to opt for one of the extremes, either separating faith and the love of God from the rest of one's life, or simply making the religious dimension indistinguishable from the rest of life and from concern for the world. The more difficult but genuine task of Christians is to maintain the "unity-in-distinction" of the love of God and the love of neighbor. For, as in the great parable of the Gospel of Matthew (25:31–46), when we have given food and drink to the hungry, clothed the naked, and visited the sick and prisoners, we have indeed ministered to Christ himself. And as the First Letter of John points out, "Those who do not love a brother or sister whom they have seen, cannot love God whom they have not seen" (4:20). Who is my neighbor? See Luke 10:29–37. Who is my brother? See Genesis 4:1–16. My neighbor, my sister, my brother is everyone, especially those most in need. And my neighbor, my sister, my brother is Christ.

The need to clarify the relationship of Christians with the world was recognized at the Second Vatican Council, though not in the initial stages of planning for the council. At first, there were no plans to issue a document specifically on the Church in the world. But after the opening of the official deliberations, a number of bishops called for such a statement, and the council as a whole and the pope agreed. There was recognition that a comprehensive presentation about the Church would have to address both the "inner life" of the Church *(ecclesia ad intra)* and the "outer" life of the Church *(ecclesia ad extra)*, both communion and mission. Thus we have two major documents (constitutions) of the council pertaining directly to the Church: *Lumen Gentium* and *Gaudium et Spes.*

This is not the place for a detailed study of *GS*. Rather, we wish to simply point out here the general vision regarding the Church-world relationship presented in that document. One of the most striking elements to be noticed is the frequent and insistent declaration that being a Christian does not diminish but on the contrary increases our responsibility for developing the world and working for justice. Consider the following references:

> Hence it is clear that men are not deterred by the Christian message from building up the world, or impelled to neglect the welfare of their fellows, but that they are rather more stringently bound to do these very things. (#34)
>
> The expectation of a new earth must not weaken but rather stimulate our concern for cultivating this one. For here grows the body of a new human family, a body which even now is able to give some kind of foreshadowing of the new age.
>
> Hence, while earthly progress must be carefully distinguished from the growth of Christ's kingdom, to the extent that the former can contribute to the better ordering of human society, it is of vital concern to the Kingdom of God. (#39)
>
> It is a mistake to think that, because we have here no lasting city, but seek the city which is to come, we are entitled to shirk our earthly responsibilities; this is to forget that by our faith we are bound all the more to fulfill these responsibilities according to the vocation of each one. . . . One of the gravest errors of our time is the dichotomy between the faith which many profess and the practice of their daily lives. . . . The Christian who shirks his temporal duties shirks his duties towards his neighbor, neglects God himself, and endangers his eternal salvation. (#43)

Why is there such an insistence in this document that Christians are even more responsible than others for the proper development of the world? We suspect that it is because of a realization that Christians and the Church had often been perceived in the immediately previous generations of separating religious faith from the affairs and challenges of life in this world. *Gaudium et Spes* decisively rejects such a dualism.

At the same time, this document clearly does not reduce Christian faith to a humanitarian spirit or reduce the Church to a merely social or political organization. Thus:

> Christ did not bequeath to the Church a mission in the political, economic, or social order: the purpose he assigned to it was a religious one. . . . By its nature and mission the Church is universal in that it is not committed to any one culture or to any political, economic, or social system. (#42)

The Church remains a sign of transcendence in the world, pointing to our ultimate destiny with God. Nonetheless, the Church, as we have seen, is a sacrament, a sign and instrument of communion with God and of unity among all people (this teaching of *LG*, #9 is repeated in *GS*, #42). In the very act of carrying out its mission, the Church "stimulates and advances human and civic culture" (*GS*, #58).

Subsequent Church documents and theological literature have attempted to maintain the fine balance, the "unity-in-distinction," articulated in *GS* between the Church's contribution to human progress and development on earth (the temporal order) and the Gospel's message about our ultimate destiny of communion with God (the eternal order). Depending on the circumstances of a given time, though, the balance seems to tilt slightly to one side or the other. Thus, for example, a synod of the world's bishops in 1971 declared in *JW*:

> It thus appears to us that an active engagement on behalf of justice and a cooperation in the transformation of the world is indeed a constitutive dimension of the proclamation of the Gospel, specifically of the mission of the Church for the

salvation and liberation of humanity from whatever situations of oppression.

Some fifteen years later, in a document examining liberation theology, the Congregation for the Doctrine of the Faith returned to this same issue but in a tone that is more attentive to the distinction of the two aspects of mission:

> Thus if the Church declares itself for the advancement of justice in human society or encourages the lay faithful to exert themselves there according to their vocation, she is not abandoning her mission. However, she is mindful of the fact that this mission is not primarily directed by and cannot be reduced to concern for the temporal order. For that reason she maintains very clearly and with great care the unity as well as the difference between evangelization and human progress: the unity, because she seeks the good of all humanity; the difference, because these two tasks are part of her mission for different reasons.
>
> (*Instruction on Christian Freedom and Liberation [ICFL], #64*)

The mission of the Church is to advance the "integral perfection of the human person" (*GS*, #59). Liberation from injustice and the progress of society on earth are part of God's plan of salvation for the human family. At the same time, there is a distinctly religious and Christian vision of human development. Indeed, our claim is that only the Christian message, the Gospel, presents the full truth about the human situation.

What Is the "World"?

In chapter five we spoke at some length about the evangelization of cultures before stepping back to look a bit more closely at what the word "culture" means. In a similar fashion, it might be helpful now, after speaking about the relationship of the Church and the world, to say just a bit more about what we mean when we say "world."

The meaning of the term "world" is not as obvious as it might seem. There is a twofold meaning to this word as used in a religious context. From the perspective of several prominent New Testament references, the "world" has a negative connotation. For example, the First Letter of John tells us:

> Do not love the world or the things in the world. The love of the Father is not in those who love the world; for all that is in the world—the desire of the flesh, the desire of the eyes, the pride in riches—comes not from the Father but from the world. (2:15–16)

Likewise, Paul says something similar to the Romans: "Do not be conformed to this world, but be transformed by the renewing of your minds." (12:2).

Biblical scholars tell us that in these passages the term "world" is being used in a restricted sense to refer to certain aspects of our experience in this life, namely, the power of sin and the condition of fallenness in humanity. Sin and evil are realities that cannot be naively brushed aside; even as we speak of our commitment to human progress and development, we should not expect the power of sin and evil to vanish. Indeed, the twentieth century tragically demonstrated that we can have no such expectation. Only at the point when God brings history to its consummation (in the eschaton) can we hope to be fully liberated from the power of sin and evil.

It may well be that the temptation to dualism in Christianity stems at least in part from these negative references to the "world" in the New Testament. But at the same time, there is a positive meaning that must be expressed. Christianity is, after all, the religion of an incarnate God, a God who becomes flesh and dwells in our world. And, after all, this is God's world, created wholly as a gift, the world that God so loved that he gave his only Son (see John 3:16).

Thus, it is wrong to consider the world as merely secular or profane, and the Church as simply sacred or holy. The world has a religious dimension from the beginning; it is graced by God in the very act of being created. What else can we consider the world but a pure gift from God? The "new creation," the "new heavens and new earth" of which the New Testament speaks and for which we hope, will not be something absolutely different from what we experience now; it will be this very world brought to the destiny that God intends for it. And even now, since the resurrection of Christ, we have, according to Paul (Romans 8:18–25) the "first fruits of the Spirit," the beginning of the transformation of this world into the promised new creation. Still, it is only now a beginning; Paul says that the "whole creation" is "groaning" to be fully liberated from sin and evil.

We are challenged to think of ourselves not just as the stewards or caretakers of the created world but also as God's created co-creators, collaborating with God in the building of the "city of God." Thus, our work in this world is not merely a means of survival, much less a curse for original sin. Rather, it contributes to the coming of the new creation. Certainly we are not creators in the same way that God is. But a number of contemporary thinkers, including Pope John Paul II in his encyclical *On Human Labor (Laborem Exercens, LE)*, have begun to speak of humans as the "created co-creators."

The World—Created for the Church

We can say that the world is created for the Church. This line of thought is expressed in the *CCC*:

> Christians of the first centuries said, "The world was created for the sake of the Church." God created the world for the sake of communion with his divine life, a communion brought about by the "convocation" of men in Christ, and this

"convocation" is the Church. The Church is the goal of all things. . . . (#760)

The Church can be thought of as that part of the world that is consciously aware of what God offers the whole human family and the entire created universe, namely, an overflowing communion of life and love. As Christians, though, we are not to experience our faith as a gift to be kept to and for ourselves. As Pope John Paul II has exclaimed, "Faith is strengthened when it is given to others!" (*RM*, #2). Our mission is to make the whole world aware of God's gifts. This, again, is why we can speak of the Church as "the universal sacrament of salvation." The Church both expresses or signifies the salvation God wants for the whole world, and in so doing brings about or effects that very salvation.

A number of the fathers of the Church referred to the Church as the "transfigured world," meaning that the Church represents what the whole world is destined to become. Of course, the historically existing Church is itself "always in need of purification," following constantly "the way of penance and renewal" (*LG*, #8). The Church experiences both the positive and the negative aspects of the world; as such it, too, must be liberated from all the forces that inhibit communion.

So when we say that the mission of the Church involves the "Christian animation of the temporal order," or the "penetration of the temporal order by the Gospel," we are saying that the world should become more and more what God has always intended it to be. In the complete fulfillment of God's plan, the "world" and the "Church" will be identical. More precisely, both the world and the Church, as we know these things, will pass away; everything will be transformed into a new creation, the "New Jerusalem," the heavenly city spoken of in the Book of Revelation.

Catholic Social Teaching— Our Best Kept Secret

The vision developed above is very lofty. We may be daunted by our weaknesses. But we must strive to translate this vision into practical teaching and action. Over the course of the past 100-plus years, there has been developing in the Church a body of thought known as Catholic social teaching, or Catholic social doctrine. Correspondingly, there has been a flourishing of programs and associations, at the local, regional, national, and universal levels, to put this teaching into practice. Readers may be familiar, for example, with organizations such as Catholic Relief Services (through which the church of the United States comes to the aid of peoples around the world), the Catholic Campaign for Human Development (which addresses situations of need within the U.S.), and local Catholic Charities offices. These are just three of the many organizations trying to serve the Church's mission of transforming the world.

The work of such organizations flows from the Catholic vision of a justly ordered world. The basic principles of that vision are spelled out in Catholic social teaching. This body of thought represents the consciousness of the whole Church striving to carry out its mission in the world. Among the principal expressions of Catholic social teaching are a series of papal documents (the social encyclicals) as well as other forms of magisterial teaching (for example, the pastoral letters of the U.S. bishops on the economy and on war and peace published in the 1980s). These documents distill and express the experience of the whole Church living in the world. They attempt to evaluate various social issues and propose Gospel-inspired ("faith-based") principles for addressing the issues. They are not the only source of moral insight in the Church; still, they represent a uniquely authoritative source of teaching with which all members of the Church should be familiar.

But too many members of the Church are not familiar with Catholic social teaching and do not sufficiently put the Gospel into practice in the world. Religious educators, as leaders in the formation of people according to the Gospel, need to become familiar with Catholic social teaching. There are a number of brief pastoral statements recently issued by the National Conference of Catholic Bishops that distill the core principles of social doctrine and provide a vision for its implementation. These short statements are much more accessible and readable than the often lengthy and technical papal social encyclicals. All of the documents that we will refer to are available on the Web site of the conference (http://www.nccbuscc.org).

A statement of particular importance is *Sharing Catholic Social Teaching: Challenges and Directions*. Approved in 1998, this statement responds to the need to more effectively integrate Catholic social teaching into the various educational ministries of the Church. The text notes that

> many Catholics do not adequately understand that the social teaching of the Church is an essential part of Catholic faith. This poses a serious challenge for all Catholics, since it weakens our capacity to be a Church that is true to the demands of the Gospel. (p. 3)

This statement summarizes the core principles of Catholic social teaching. Seven themes are presented:

1. **Life and Dignity of the Human Person:** "Our belief in the sanctity of human life and the inherent dignity of the human person is the foundation of all the principles of our social teaching."

2. **Call to Family, Community, and Participation:** "In a global culture driven by excessive individualism, our tradition proclaims that the person is not only sacred but also social."

3. **Rights and Responsibilities:** "Every person has a fundamental right to life and a right to those things required for human decency. Corresponding to these rights are duties and responsibilities—to one another, to our families, and to the larger society."

4. **Option for the Poor and Vulnerable:** "In a world characterized by growing prosperity for some and pervasive poverty for others, Catholic teaching proclaims that a basic moral test is how our most vulnerable members are faring."

5. **The Dignity of Work and the Rights of Workers:** "Work is more than a way to make a living; it is a form of continuing participation in God's creation. If the dignity of work is to be protected, then the basic rights of workers must be respected—the right to productive work, to decent and fair wages, to organize and join unions, to private property, and to economic initiative."

6. **Solidarity:** "Catholic social teaching proclaims that we are our brothers' and sisters' keepers, wherever they live. We are one human family, whatever our national, racial, ethnic, economic, and ideological differences."

7. **Care for God's Creation:** "On a planet conflicted over environmental issues, the Catholic tradition insists that we show our respect for the Creator by our stewardship of creation. Care for the earth is not just an Earth Day slogan, it is a requirement of our faith." (pgs. 4–6)

There are several other important statements. *Living the Gospel of Life: A Challenge to American Catholics* (1998) provides guidance for developing the virtues needed to cultivate a "culture of life" in our society. *Called to Global Solidarity: International Challenges for U.S. Parishes* (1997) calls on Catholic communities in the United States to reach beyond their own parochial borders and our own national borders to live in solidarity and justice with the peoples of the world.

The statement *Faithful Citizenship: Civic Responsibility for a New Millennium* (1999) provides a framework for members of the Church in the United States to participate in the political process in the election cycle of the year 2000 and beyond. Finally, *Everyday Christianity: To Hunger and Thirst for Justice* (1998) is "a pastoral reflection on lay discipleship for justice in a new millennium." This statement highlights "one essential dimension of the lay vocation that is sometimes overlooked or neglected: the social mission of Christians in the world" (p. 1).

Summary

In everyday activity, in ways great and small, all of us are called to make our contribution to the building of a more just and peaceful world. As we move into the new millennium, beginning with the celebration of the Jubilee Year, we renew our commitment to follow Christ and "bring good news to the poor . . . to proclaim release to the captives and recovery of sight to the blind, to let the oppressed go free" (Luke 4:18). *Everyday Christianity* ends with a "Jubilee Pledge for Charity, Justice, and Peace." We shall let this pledge stand as the summary of this chapter.

As disciples of Jesus in the new millennium, I/We pledge to:

* **Pray** regularly for greater justice and peace.

* **Learn** more about Catholic social teaching and its call to protect human life, stand with the poor, and care for creation.

* **Reach** across boundaries of religion, race, ethnicity, gender, and disabling conditions.

* **Live** justly in family life, school, work, the marketplace, and the political arena.

* **Serve** those who are poor and vulnerable, sharing more time and talent.

* **Give** more generously to those in need at home and abroad.

- **Advocate** public policies that protect human life, promote human dignity, preserve God's creation, and build peace.

- **Encourage** others to work for greater charity, justice, and peace. (pp. 14–15)

FOR REFLECTION

1. How do you understand the call to be "in the world but not of the world"?

2. How does your faith community equip its members to effectively carry out the Church's mission in the world?

3. In what concrete ways do you apply Catholic social teaching now? In what ways could you promote a more widespread understanding and application of Catholic social teaching?

CHAPTER 7

The Church—
One, Holy,
Catholic, and
Apostolic

We began these reflections on the Church by referring to the experience of celebrating the eucharistic Liturgy. A consideration of this most basic act of the Church, the event in which we most deeply realize our Christian identity, provides us with the main themes around which to construct a theology of the Church, that is, an ecclesiology. The interplay of gathering and being sent, of coming together and going forth, of communion and mission, is a basic rhythm of the Christian life. In the preceding chapters, we have attempted to spell out some of the details of a vision of the Church based on this rhythm.

Another element of the eucharistic Liturgy is the profession of faith that we make when reciting the creed. Our shared confession of belief in the triune God binds us to one another and helps to both express and create communion among members of the Church. In making this profession of faith, we state our belief that the Church is "one, holy, catholic, and apostolic." These have traditionally been regarded as the marks of the Church, that is, its essential characteristics.

Many studies of ecclesiology are organized according to these four themes. In this book, we have not made specific reference to the one, holy, catholic, and apostolic Church. But that does not mean that the themes of unity, sanctity, catholicity, and apostolicity have been absent from our reflections. On the contrary, in studying the communion and mission of the Church, we have thoroughly and explicitly taken account of its oneness and apostolicity. Obviously, to speak of communion is to talk about the oneness of the Church. Likewise, we have seen that the most basic meaning of "apostolic" is "being sent," thus pointing to the Church's missionary identity. But to be apostolic also recalls the themes of communion and oneness, reminding us that responsibility for the unity of the Church has been historically entrusted to bishops, those ministers regarded as successors of the original apostles. We have addressed what makes the Church "one" and "apostolic," therefore, in the previous chapters.

What has been less obvious, though not absent, is explicit attention to the holiness and catholicity of the Church. Thus, it seems fitting in this final chapter to offer some further remarks on the Church as "holy" and "catholic." We may understand holiness and catholicity to be attributes that pertain to communion, so that, to be more specific, the Church is a "holy communion" and a "catholic communion." When we recall also that the purpose of mission is to make our communion richer and more inclusive, we can see that communion or oneness is in some sense the fundamental characteristic of the Church. Sanctity, catholicity, and apostolicity are further specifications of communion. So we may likewise recall that, in the end, when full communion among divine and human persons is accomplished, there will be no further need for mission.

The Church—Holy in a Way
That Can Never Fail

We believe that the Church is holy. But what does it mean to be holy? And how can the Church be, as we have seen, at once holy and in need of purification? Is there a distinction between the holiness of the Church as such and the holiness of its individual members?

To begin with, holiness, properly speaking, belongs to God alone. As we sing in the Gloria, "You alone are the Holy One." The earliest sense of the word "holy" (*hagios* in Greek, *sanctus* in Latin) is "set apart," that is, God and what belongs to God is clearly marked off from everything else, which remains "profane." There seemed to be a particular need in the biblical period to emphasize the "otherness" of God as compared to created things, so as to preserve the sense that God is not to be confused with the forces of nature or the handiworks of human beings.

But the holiness of God, which inspires awe and worship, can be shared with or imparted to human persons and created things. Thus the Bible describes God's desire to form a "holy nation, a people set apart." Holiness is attributed to everything that is consecrated to the service and worship of God: to the Temple, to the books of Scripture, to priests. Principally, however, it is the people as a whole—the community of Israel in the Old Testament, the Christian Church in the New Testament—that is called to be holy, that is, to be God's people. But the choosing and setting apart of these people by God are not an act of favoritism or elitism; rather, these people are to be an explicit sign ("sacrament") of the relationship that God wishes to establish with all peoples.

The Church is holy first of all because its people are God's people. Paul speaks of the Church as both the "body of Christ" and the "temple of the Spirit." This holiness, though, is both a gift and a task. Paul addresses the Corinthians as "those who are sanctified in Christ Jesus" who are at the same time "called to be saints" (1 Corinthians 1:2). The Ephesians are told that "you are no longer strangers and aliens, but you are citizens with the saints and also members of the household of God." (Ephesians 2:19). Christians have been made holy, but they are also called to become holy.

Holiness, then, is properly said of the Church because of the holiness of Christ and the Spirit, who form and animate us as a community of people. In this sense, the Church can never not be holy. According to *LG*, the Church is "unfailingly holy" (#39). To be more technical, it is sometimes said that the Church is "indefectible" in its holiness. We believe this because of the promise of Christ that the Spirit will keep the Church faithful to the message of the Gospel (see John 16:13, for example). On this basis, we also believe that there are gifts given to the Church that will remain holy even if we use them in an unworthy way. The books of Scripture, the sacraments, and other gifts of the Spirit are in themselves always holy because of their source.

The Holiness of the Church— Genuine Though Imperfect

But this holy Church is also sinful. Thus it must constantly follow "the path of penance and renewal." But how can a thing be holy and sinful at the same time? Isn't this like saying that a drink could be both hot and cold?

The Church is a communion of people joined to Christ by the action of the Holy Spirit. Insofar as Christ is the head of this body of people and the Holy Spirit is its heart or soul, then, of course, the Church is holy. But we human members of the Church are far from perfect; we all sin and fall short of the life to which God is calling us. Often enough, of course, we as individuals and groups within the Church fail to be holy; and in these cases we do not necessarily impute to the Church as a whole the failings of some of its members. But again, we all pray, "Forgive us our trespasses." Furthermore, sometimes it is clearly the Church as a whole that appears to bear responsibility for attitudes and actions incompatible with the Gospel.

The Jubilee of the Year 2000 called the Church to a collective examination of conscience. According to Pope John Paul II's letter *On the Coming of the Third Millennium (Tertio Millennio Adveniente, TMA)*, which outlines the preparations for this celebration:

> . . . the Church should become more fully conscious of the sinfulness of her children, recalling all those times in history when they departed from the spirit of Christ and his Gospel and, instead of offering to the world the witness of a life inspired by the values of faith, indulged in ways of thinking and acting which were truly *forms of counter-witness and scandal.*
>
> (#33, emphasis added)

Among the "painful chapter[s] of history to which the sons and daughters of the Church must return with a spirit of repentance," this letter recalls sins that have wounded Christian unity, such as "*intolerance and even the use of violence* in the service of truth" (#35). But it is not only historical sins of which we must repent; the present time "also presents not a few shadows," that is, evil situations, for which Christians share responsibility. Examples include the loss of respect for life and the family, violations of human rights, and "grave forms of injustice and exclusion." "It must be asked how many Christians really know and put into practice the principles of the Church's social doctrine" (#36). To use a traditional terminology, Christians must confess both sins of commission and sins of omission, that is, "what I have done and what I have failed to do."

Obviously, "indefectably holy" cannot simply mean "perfectly holy." To call the Church holy does not mean that there are no defects or sins among its members but, rather, that the Church as a whole will never fall away from the Gospel to such an extent that it loses the possibility of repentance and conversion. As long as we have the Gospel as the mirror in which to examine ourselves, we have hope that we may more fully become what we are called to be, that is, God's holy people.

In a way, the juxtaposition of holiness and sinfulness in the Church actually highlights the extent to which God loves us. In the painful experience of moral failure, we realize just how abounding is God's mercy and compassion. Paradoxically, we are called to exchange our sinfulness for Christ's holiness. Christ becomes sin! "God made the one who did not know sin to be sin" in order that we might become holy. Just as in a marriage, husband and wife give to each other everything about themselves, both gifts and shortcomings, so in our union with Christ we give him everything we are, including our weakness and failure, and we in turn receive his life. So the intimate love of Christ and the Church is as that of husband and wife, as the Letter to the Ephesians proclaims (5:21–33).

Lumen Gentium teaches that God calls everyone to holiness:

> Thus it is evident to everyone, that all the faithful of Christ of whatever rank or status, are called to the fullness of the Christian life and to the perfection of charity; by this holiness as such a more human manner of living is promoted in this earthly society. (#40)

Charity is "the first and most necessary gift" of the Holy Spirit; it is the "bond of perfection," the "fullness of the law" (#42). Charity is superior to all other virtues; indeed, it is the very "form" of all the virtues. Clearly, holiness consists above all in the love of God and our neighbor. "On these two commandments hang all the law and the prophets" (see Matthew 22:34–40). Thus, "It is the love of God and the love of one's neighbor which points out the true disciple of Christ" (*LG*, #42).

The Catholic Unity of the Church

We turn now to a consideration of the catholicity of the Church. Almost all Christians, and not just those who belong to the Roman Catholic Church, profess belief in the "catholic Church." By a widely followed convention, we use "catholic" (lower case) when referring to that quality of the Church spoken of in the creed, and "Catholic" (upper case) when referring to the Roman Catholic Church (that is, all those churches in communion with the church in Rome; these include Eastern rite Catholic Churches as well as the Church of the Latin rite).

In this section, we wish to focus on the Church as catholic, which practically all Christians confess. What does this mean? Our term derives originally from the Greek *katholikos*, meaning "according to the whole" or "universal." As the adjective "catholic" began to be applied to the noun "church" in a number of early Christian writings, several different nuances of meaning came to emerge, reflecting various facets of universality or fullness. There was the plain meaning of geographical extension; the Church is catholic in that it is spread (or is in the process of spreading) across the world. There is the sense of oneness that was emphasized by the term "catholic"; to be truly catholic, the Church must be one Church throughout the world.

Another important dimension of catholicity appears in the second century in the need to distinguish genuine or orthodox Christian communities from various heretical and schismatic sects. Conflicting interpretations of the Gospel resulted in contradictory beliefs and practices, and early Christians gradually developed norms or touchstones ("rules of faith," such as early baptismal and catechetical formulas) to judge what was truly Christian. In this sense catholic came to mean the opposite of sectarian or factional. Finally, catholic came to also denote the idea of fullness or plenitude, meaning a rich diversity that is reconciled into unity.

In the subsequent history of Christianity, there have been numerous attempts to define more precisely the catholic dimension of the Church. That task has been made more difficult by the internal divisions of Christianity into Catholic, Orthodox, and Protestant branches, with further disunity within each branch. And practically all of these Christians, as we have said, believe in the catholic Church, although many are not Catholic. The Catholic Church acknowledges that it cannot simply identify Christ's Church with itself or with any other ecclesial body. According to *LG*,

> The one Church of Christ which in the Creed is professed as one, holy, catholic and apostolic. . . . subsists in the Catholic Church, which is governed by the successor of Peter and by the Bishops in communion with him, although many elements of sanctification and of truth are found outside its visible structure. (#8)

There has been much speculation about the meaning of "subsists in," which the council used instead of "exists in." In the context of *LG* and other documents, this choice of terms seems to indicate that the one Church of Christ, while most fully manifest in the Catholic Church, embraces in some way the Orthodox Churches and the Churches and ecclesial communities stemming from the Protestant Reformation. All of these bodies are linked in a "real though imperfect" communion. The council's document on ecumenism, *UR*, offers further reflection on this wider ecclesial communion:

> Moreover, some, even very many, of the most significant elements and endowments which together go to build up and give life to the Church itself, can exist outside the visible boundaries of the Catholic

Church: the written Word of God; the life of grace; faith, hope, and charity, with the other interior gifts of the Holy Spirit, and visible elements too. All of these, which come from Christ and lead back to Christ, belong by right to the one Church of Christ. Nevertheless , . . . it is only through Christ's Catholic Church, which is "the all-embracing means of salvation," that they can benefit fully from the means of salvation (#3).

The text maintains a distinction between "the Church itself" or "the one Church of Christ" and "the Catholic Church." At the same time, it teaches that the "fullness of the means of salvation" is found only in the Catholic Church. As we have seen, the principal means for building up ecclesial communion are the ministries of Word, sacrament, and pastoral leadership. If the fullness of these means is present only in the Catholic Church, still, very many means are found in other Christian communities.

But the "one Church of Christ" is more than the means to communion; it is also and more fundamentally the fruit of communion. This Church is the communion of persons to which all Christians belong in some greater or lesser degree. However, some Christians belonging to churches with less than the full means of communion are living a more profound life of Christian faith, hope, and charity than are some Catholic Christians, whose church does possess the full means of communion. That is why we cannot simply identify the "one Church of Christ" in an absolute way with the Catholic Church, even though the Catholic Church alone possesses the fullness of the means of salvation.

Catholicity—The Fullness of Giving and Receiving

Contemporary observations about catholicity include the several senses of the term that we mentioned above that develop the idea of universality or wholeness. Especially prominent in recent reflections is an emphasis on catholicity as the fullness of the sharing of goods among all peoples. This means that the Church is truly catholic when it embraces every culture and every group of people, reconciling all the diverse resources, charisms, and goods in the world into unity. Recall that when we discussed the evangelization of cultures, we saw that one reason the Gospel must be brought to all cultures is to make the Church more truly catholic. The word "plenitude" is another term that is sometimes used to refer to the rich complementarity of gifts that should come together to make up the whole Church. This is the sense given in *LG*:

> By reason of [this characteristic of universality], the Catholic Church strives constantly and with due effect to bring all humanity and all its possessions back to its source in Christ, with Him as its head and united in His Spirit. In virtue of this catholicity each part contributes through its special gifts to the good of the other parts and of the whole Church. Through the common sharing of gifts and through the common effort to attain to fullness in unity, the whole and each of the pats receive increase (#13).

We might say that the Church is catholic only because Christ himself is catholic. In several references, especially in the Letters to the Ephesians and Colossians, Christ is spoken of in terms of "fullness." These references indicate that Christ embraces or "takes to himself" every dimension of our existence, so that all things might be "reconciled" in him. Precisely because all things were created through him, Christ is the one in whom all things find their true place. By becoming human, Christ "assumed" everything about our lives.

Jesus was a truly "catholic person." By this we mean he was totally open to others; his personality was such that he related to all other persons and to the whole world in an inclusive way. Nothing good was alien or foreign to him. Jesus embraced everything about being human. We are called in our own way to become "catholic persons," that is, persons who are fully open to the mutual exchange of gifts with all other persons in the world. So the catholic Church is that community of persons in Christ who are constituted by this mutual giving and receiving of gifts, this sharing of all that is good in God's creation. An image that comes to mind is a choir or symphony: Each person contributes something unique that is brought into a greater harmony by the director or conductor. Christ is the great conductor; in him all things find their beauty.

Summary

From the above reflections, we can see that being one, holy, catholic, and apostolic is both something that the Church *is*, and something that the Church is continually called to *become*. Our gift is also our task. The Church is what it is first of all because it shares in the unity, sanctity, catholicity, and apostolicity of God. God is one. God is holy. God is catholic, that is, the fullness of being. And God is apostolic in that Christ and the Spirit are sent into the world. The Church receives all these qualities from the triune God. We are called to measure up to the gifts we have received. And that is our great challenge and adventure!

For Reflection

1. When you think of the Church as "holy," what comes to mind? When you think of the Church as "sinful," what comes to mind?

2. Why is it important to distinguish between the "Catholic Church" and the "one Church of Christ"?

3. In what ways could both you and the Church become more "catholic"?

Conclusion

We have come full circle in this study. Communion leads to mission, and mission leads back to communion. Our experiences as Christians "in" the Church, especially in the eucharistic Liturgy, and our experiences of life "in the world" are crucial ingredients of this book. In the Liturgy, as we gather, hear the Word of God, profess the creed, celebrate the Eucharist, and are commissioned for service, we affirm for ourselves and others what it means to be Church. In the world, as we seek peace, work for justice, defend the dignity of life, strengthen our families, and care for the earth, we affirm for ourselves and others what it means to be Church.

A vision of Church has been spelled out in the words of this book. But the words must become flesh for the vision to be realized. We all are called, in a rich diversity of ways, to embody in our lives the Word of God, the Gospel. We are not just called to *belong* to the Church; we are called to *be* the Church. We are called to communion and mission, to gathering and being sent, to coming together and going forth. Let us live this gift with gratitude, joy, and the hope of that future gathering in which the banquet of celebration will know no end.

Abbreviations

AA   *Apostolicam Actuositatem (Decree on the Apostolate of Lay People)*

AGD   *Ad Gentes Divinitus (Decree on the Church's Missionary Activity)*

CCC   *Catechism of the Catholic Church*

CD   *Christus Dominus (Decree on the Pastoral Office of Bishops in the Church)*

CL   *Christifideles Laici (On the Vocation and the Mission of the Lay Faithful in the Church and in the World)*

DV   *Dei Verbum (Dogmatic Constitution on Divine Revelation)*

EN   *Evangelii Nuntiandi (On Evangelization in the Modern World)*

FC   *Familiaris Consortio (On the Role of the Christian Family in the Modern World)*

GCD   *General Catechetical Directory* (1971)

GDC   *General Directory for Catechesis* (1997)

GMD   *Go and Make Disciples*

GS   *Gaudium et Spes (Pastoral Constitution on the Church in the Modern World)*

ICFL   *Instruction on Christian Freedom and Liberation*

JW   *Justice in the World*

LG   *Lumen Gentium (Dogmatic Constitution on the Church)*

MD   *Mulieris Dignitatem (On the Dignity and Vocation of Women)*

PO   *Presbyterorum Ordinis (Decree on the Ministry and Life of Priests)*

RCIA Rite of Christian Initiation of Adults

RH   *Redemptor Hominis (The Redeemer of Man)*

RM   *Redemptoris Missio (On the Permanent Validity of the Church's Missionary Mandate)*

SC   *Sacrosanctum Concilium (Constitution on the Sacred Liturgy)*

TMA   *Tertio Millennio Adveniente (On the Coming of the Third Millennium)*

UR   *Unitatis Redintegratio (Decree on Ecumenism)*

Resources for Further Study

Many of the Church documents cited in this book can be found on the Web sites of the Vatican (http://www. vatican.va) and the National Conference of Catholic Bishops/United States Catholic Conference (http://www. nccbuscc.org). Among the many books on the Church, the following are recommended.

Braxton, Edward. *The Faith Community. One, Holy, Catholic, and Apostolic.* Notre Dame, IN: Ave Maria Press, 1990.
    A popular introduction to the study of the Church, written by a noted African-American theologian and bishop.

Donovan, Daniel. *The Church as Idea and Fact.* Collegeville, MN: Michael Glazier Books. The Liturgical Press, 1988.
    A good selection for adult education groups, this short book should be quite accessible for the average reader.

Dulles, Avery. *Models of the Church* (expanded edition). New York: Image Books, 1991.
    A modern "classic" of ecclesiology, recently updated. Dulles presents six major models for understanding the Church: the Church as institution, mystical communion, sacrament, herald, servant, and community of disciples.

Dulles, Avery, and Patrick Granfield. *The Theology of the Church: A Bibliography.* New York: Paulist Press, 1999.
    This is the most complete available listing of books and articles about the Church. It is organized according to fifty-three distinct themes, so it is relatively easy to find material on practically any particular aspect of the Church.

Flannery, Austin, OP, ed. *Vatican Council II: The Conciliar and Post Conciliar Documents*. Northport, NY: Costello Publishing Company, 1998.

One of the better translations of the conciliar documents. Includes study questions.

Garijo-Guembe, Miguel. *Communion of the Saints: Foundation, Nature, and Structure of the Church*. Collegeville, MN: The Liturgical Press, 1994.

This is a challenging but very rich book by a European scholar. Of all the texts listed in this appendix, it is the one that is most similar in outlook to the present book.

Lawler, Michael G., and Thomas J. Shanahan. *Church: A Spirited Communion*. Collegeville, MN: The Liturgical Press, 1995.

An engaging reflection on various aspects of the Church as communion—graced, prophetic, sacramental, and ministerial communion. Also contains an excellent discussion of the relationship between laity and hierarchy in the Church. This book develops the "communion ecclesiology" of the Second Vatican Council.

McBrien, Richard. *Responses to 101 Questions on the Church*. New York: Paulist Press, 1996.

A well-known commentator on the Church offers an accessible guide to questions on every major aspect of the mystery of the Church: its nature, mission, ministries, and structures.

McPartlan, Paul. *Sacrament of Salvation: An Introduction to Eucharistic Ecclesiology*. Edinburgh: T&T Clark, 1995.

A relatively short book that gives an excellent presentation to eucharistic ecclesiology. It is a shorter and more popular version of the author's doctoral dissertation. He especially draws on the thought of the great twentieth-century Catholic theologian Henri de Lubac, as well as the contemporary Orthodox theologian John Zizoulas.

Orsy, Ladislas. *The Church Learning and Teaching*. Wilmington, DE: Michael Glazier, 1987.

A popular and highly informative essay on the ways in which the entire Church makes progress in its understanding of the Gospel. Explains the teaching office of the magisterium and the role of other Church teachers.

Sullivan, Francis A., SJ. *The Church We Believe In: One, Holy, Catholic, and Apostolic*. Mahwah, NJ: Paulist Press, 1988.

A meticulously thorough, precise, and illuminating study of the Church by a foremost American scholar. This book is widely used in seminary courses on ecclesiology. Among its many strengths is its careful reading and explanation of many important passages from official Church documents, especially those of the Second Vatican Council.

Tillard, Jean-Marie R. *Church of Churches: The Ecclesiology of Communion*. Collegeville, MN: The Liturgical Press, 1992.

A comprehensive and scholarly study of communion ecclesiology with special attention to its ecumenical implications.

Acknowledgments

The Scripture quotations contained herein are from the New Revised Standard Version Bible, Catholic edition copyright © 1993 and 1989 by the Division of Christian Education of the National Council of the Churches of Christ in the U.S.A. Used by permission. All rights reserved.

Excerpts from Vatican conciliar, post-conciliar and papal documents are from the official translations, Libreria Editrice Vaticana, 00120 Citta del Vaticano.

Excerpts from the *General Directory for Catechesis*, copyright © 1997 Libreria Editrice Vaticana—United States Catholic Conference, Inc. Used with permission. All rights reserved.

Excerpts from the English translation of the *Catechism of the Catholic Church for the United States of America*, copyright © 1994, United States Catholic Conference, Inc.—Libreria Editrice Vaticana. English translation of *Catechism of the Catholic Church: Modifications from the Editio Typica* copyright © 1997, United States Catholic Conference, Inc.—Used with permission.

Excerpts from *Go and Make Disciples* copyright © 1993 United States Catholic Conference, Inc. (USCC), Washington, D.C.; excerpts from *Sharing Catholic Social Teaching* copyright © 1998 USCC; excerpts from *Everyday Christianity* copyright © 1998 USCC. Used with permission. All rights reserved. No portion of these documents may be reproduced by any means without permission in writing from the copyright owner.

About the Author

Morris Pelzel is assistant professor of systematic theology at Saint Meinrad School of Theology, St. Meinrad, Indiana. He received a Ph.D. in theology from the Catholic University of America in 1994. He teaches a broad variety of courses at Saint Meinrad, including foundational theology, theological anthropology, Trinity, ecumenical theology, and ecclesiology. His course in science and theology was selected as an award winner in the 1997 Templeton Foundation Course Design Program in Science and Religion.